Praise for *Women Standing Strong Together*

"Sometimes in our darkest moment we find the strength to remember who we are. 'Shattered Pieces' by Gloria J Coppola speaks of the journey to surrendering to your soul's calling. It is one of self-discovery and awakening to knowing and living the truth you have always known inside. The analogy of the mosaic and colorful use of words jumped out and danced before me with magical and imaginative expression and touched me spiritually, with an unstoppable calling. Tears formed and gently rolled down my cheeks as I sat in silence feeling the raw emotion of each shattered piece of Gloria's soul as she carries you on a journey that reminds us all to trust our intuition, to follow the thirst for knowledge which can give us the peace that our soul knows we so desire."

~ Queen Kimmie 101, Author of *"How I Learned To Love and Let Go"*

"Surrendering to the Divine Plan by Deborah Marino-Finley addresses the possibility for all of us to find our way from a dark place, through observation and openness for the Divine orchestration of our life, especially when we realize life is bigger than ourselves. Her story is a great road map for personal and emotional growth."

~ Terry Davidson Jackson, Coauthor of International Best Seller *"Wild and Wise Women"*

"We are hard-wired to learn through stories. It has been part of every culture and native tradition because our brains are able to integrate the learning from stories and stories are easy to remember and thus pass on to the next generation. The stories in this book take you on a journey of transformation, but hidden within the stories are the secrets to lasting change from within. Curl up with some hot cocoa and this book to be taken on a journey through the incredible stories in this book."

- Dana Pharant, author of *"The Inner Dominatrix™ Guide: Become a Badass in Business"*

"At this amazing time in humanity when women are finally rising to their greatness and full potential "Women Standing Strong Together" inspires and shows us that each and every women has the power to transform and empower their lives however difficult the journey may seem. Jenny Pederson in her story "Not Your Mother's Guide to Supermom" delves deep into her heart and so openly tells the dilemmas of becoming a mother and keeping true to her own soul and truth. She becomes like the voice of women who was made to choose between her truth or to sacrifice herself for the role of becoming the perfect mother that is so conditioned into the psyche of every women. Her story is the courage to find her soul's desires and who she is meant to become in this world as well as being the great and loving mother she can be and that every women has the potential and the right to have it all."

- Zekiye Olgaçay, author of *"Spiritual Renaissance"*

Praise for *Women Standing Strong Together*

"When we go through hardship adversity and suffering in life, we can either fall into the abyss of victimhood or we can use life's challenges as they were intended, for us to evolve and grow. Each woman in this book made a decision in her life to fight back. The moment she made that firm decision was the moment the sun began to shine in her life again. By taking her power back, believing in herself is what gave them the strength to have a fresh outlook on life and overcome the challenges they faced."

~ Robert Crown, author of *"Suffering Ends When Awakening Begins"*

"Women Standing Strong Together" is an inspiring collection of stories from women who have battled adversity in their lives and emerged stronger as a result. I admire these authors who demonstrated true bravery in telling their truth. Each story is as unique as the woman writing it, which makes for a fascinating and compelling read from start to finish."

~ Gloria Grace Rand, Transformational Life Coach

"What a compilation of victories! This book illustrates that we do not really know the person in front of us and the struggles they have overcome. These women have each gone through tragedy and have seen themselves as whole, complete and a true gift to others by simply being their best self, unique and awesome! A lesson we all can apply to ourselves."

~ Joe Petroski, Master Healer and Performance Expert

"Women Standing Strong Together" is an amazing compilation of stories about the power, tenacity, wisdom and strength of women! Each of these women have turned tragedy into triumph and wounds healed to wholeness. How each one chose to rise above their situations is a testament to the power and possibility of new choices that lie within each one of us."

~ Sandie LeMieux, Intuitive Life & Business Strategist, Healing Arts Master, Speaker

"Remarkable stories that are so powerful and inspiring they give the reader a new outlook on life's purpose. It has motivated me to transform my own life and to embrace the learning and growth that awaits me. It has been pulling at me for years to seek more balance and peace in my life and reconnect with Reiki which years ago awakened my soul. After reading these stories I am not putting it off anymore. The time is NOW!"

~ Denise Kuhn Newborg

Women Standing Strong Together

Stories of Surrendering to Your Authentic Self

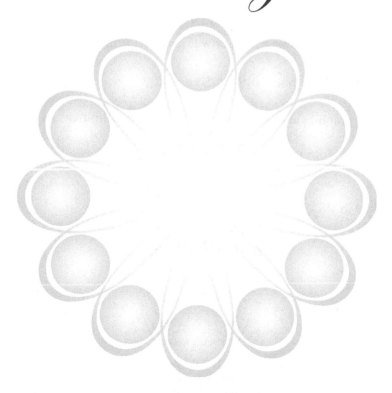

Women Standing Strong Together: Stories of Surrendering to Your Authentic Self

First published by Powerful Potential and Purpose Publishing 2019

First printing, December 2019

Cover art, graphics and book design by Candy Lyn Thomen

ISBN: 9781671987289
ISBN:

Published in USA

Powerful
Potential and Purpose

PUBLISHING

www.PPP-Publishing.com
PPP Publishing
Spokane Valley, WA 99206

This book is dedicated, with gratitude, to all of the courageous women who contributed to it's creation, along with all of the amazing people who will read it, learn from it, and benefit from the stories contained in these pages.

Life is a journey best enjoyed with the members of your tribe!

Contents

In truth there is a small one who suffers in each of us, an angel trying to grow wings in the dark, and as this angel learns how to sing, we lose the urge to hide. Indeed, when one heart speaks, all hearts fly. This is what it means to be great – to speak what feels unspeakable and have it release what waits in us all.

~ Mark Nepo, *"The Book of Awakening"*

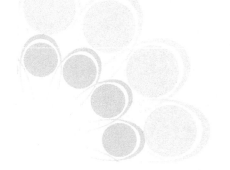

Introduction

*"It takes courage to grow up and
become who you really are."*

~ e e cummings

Giving ourselves permission to grow, to focus on our needs, to be authentic, takes a great deal of courage and a massive step to be honored, respected, and celebrated.

Have you ever felt alone? Have you thought people just don't understand you? That the journey you're taking is scary? Have you questioned life and the very essence of your purpose? Do you wish someone could relate to you?

When I was called to collaborate with a group of women in a dream, for a project called Powerful Potential and Purpose, I knew in my heart and soul I had to say YES! These women have experienced great tragedy, depression, suicidal thoughts, losses beyond imagination, and abuse that may break your heart. It is a privilege to know each of them more authentically and why they serve now.

"It's only after you've stepped out of your comfort zone that you begin to change, grow and transform."

~ Roy T. Bennett, The Light in the Heart.

Some of us are fortunate to have an inner strength, perhaps faith or courage, that helps us take one more step forward to find the truth. Others may not, because they are lost deeper in the darkness and feel completely alone, without support. There are those that crawl up, hoping and reaching out their hand, "Please help" and then help comes in many ways - a sign, an angel that crosses our path - and we rise up strong.

Brené Brown, PhD, LMSW says, "Living a brave life is not always easy: we stumble, and we fall." She asked herself when writing her book Rising Strong, "What do people have in common?" The answer was clear. We can all recognize the power of emotion. When we are not afraid to lean into the discomfort in the midst of the struggle, our courage is tested, our values confronted and we make a choice from a place of deep truth and we learn who we are.

This project has enlightened me to gain greater understanding of my soul blueprint, something we aren't taught at a young age because we are listening to earthly doctrines, beliefs and the systems we are taught. I never considered for a moment to pursue writing further or to publish books. I won awards at the age of 17 for writing. I never shared this with anyone because it didn't seem important. I was the literary editor for our school magazine and I never saw the big deal, nor did anyone else ever encourage me to pursue this direction. For forty years, I was a featured writer in many holistic magazines, wrote in coauthored books, wrote for newspapers and published four books of my own. Still, I went on to pursue other things in life. All that would play a part in this process.

Now I see how my soul was laying out the design for me and finally, by the grace of my intuition, guides, angels, and God, I am listening. You see, even e e cummings influenced me at the tender age of 15 and his quote at the beginning was already ingrained in my cells. Some of us just take longer. I am one of those.

For decades I have studied with shaman, kahuna and sages and they all ask, "Who are you? Why are you here?" They made me cry and brought me to my knees. But they also helped me gain a deeper perspective into the soul's essence, the deeper sense of our purpose. We typically say - I am a parent, a wife, teacher, author, a counselor, an accountant, a truck driver, etc. Who we are takes deep transformational unfolding, like removing the layers from an onion and revealing the lotus flower within, to yet again go deeper on this spiritual journey.

People may not understand you. They may get uncomfortable when you start to think differently. Some may attack you and leave you. Others will welcome you with open arms because there is an awakening of consciousness happening; the ones taking us home, standing strong together. We are building communities of support. We are the ones helping the next seven generations.

I invite you now to open your arms and connect with these heart-felt stories, these raw emotions, and concepts, these women who have had the courage to walk through the fire, to climb the mountain, to see something more not only in themselves but in their purpose with each other.

It is my intention that you too own the tremendous power that lies deep in your cells, that you know your potential and that you find and live your purpose and you reveal your magnificence.

"When the waves touch the sky and we ride through the light of the tunnel, then we will understand peace."

~ Gloria Coppola, author, spiritual teacher, publisher

Women Standing Strong Together

"Finding yourself is not
really how it works. You aren't a
ten-dollar bill in last winter's coat pocket.
You are also not lost. Your true self is right
there, buried under cultural conditioning,
other people's opinions, and inaccurate
conclusions you drew as a kid that became
your beliefs about who you are.
'Finding yourself' is actually returning to
yourself. An unlearning, an excavation,
a remembering who you were before
the world got its hands on you."

~Emily McDowell

Candy Lyn Thomen

Candy is a professional artist and graphic designer with over 26 years of experience. She is also an energy healer, intuitive and empath. Through her gifts she is able to connect with her clients energy, helping her create unique, Soul-based art and designs. Candy's talent can be seen throughout this book and as well as many others. In her current creative focus, she has partnered with author and spiritual coach Gloria Coppola to form Powerful Potential and Purpose Publishing. Their belief is that we each have a powerful purpose in our lives. Their vision and mission is to help authors and readers alike reach their full potential and live their soul purpose.

Candy's passion lies in creating, believing adamantly that we each are born with innate creative gifts. Her mission is to help people find that inner creative voice, regardless of what it is, and in finding that creative gift, to give fire to the passion that lies in our hearts.

www.PPP-Publishing.com / PPPPublishingUS@gmail.com
www.candylyncreates.com / candylyncreates@gmail.com

Chapter One

For the Love of Creation

Candy Lyn Thomen

The sky was brilliant blue, the small patch that I could see, but the city itself was a monochrome field of gray. The cold morning sun had not yet risen high enough to shine its warmth and light into the depths of downtown Calgary, Canada, an appropriate metaphor for the process of awakening I was about to embark upon.

"You don't always have to endure everything, you know." My friend said to me from the passenger seat as I negotiated traffic lights, morning pedestrians and my phone's GPS map while driving her to the airport.

The light ahead turned red, and we stopped. "Just because you CAN tolerate something or manage the pain, doesn't mean you have to. You have the right to say stop and to ask for what you need." We were talking about a healing session she had given me the day before. Releasing the deep, muscular tension had been intense, but it wasn't anything I couldn't handle so I had laid there allowing her to do her work, breathing through the pain. She asked multiple times if I needed her to ease up a bit. "No, it's fine" I kept telling her, just like I do in most situations

BOOM! Through the echo of her words, like a bomb going off, a realization hit me. *You have the right to say stop.*

As the light turned green, a flood of images momentarily overwhelmed me. A rapid-fire film reel beginning with the first time I was sexually abused, fast-forwarding through my life and the many times I had stood by, powerless and mute, believing I did not have the basic right to take control of my body, my circumstances, or my life. I didn't have the right to say stop.

As downtown traffic flowed and people walked across the street, the outside world once again took form and shape. I was floored by the sudden understanding of when and how I had lost my voice, my power, and my ability to stand up for myself.

After coming home from Calgary, Canada, the words rang in my head with the volume of an air raid siren. For years I had been focusing on healing the parts of myself I felt were wounded, to make a better life, deepen my relationships, be the best version of me I could be. While I was healthier and happier than I had been in a long time, there were still parts of my life and my inner world that weren't nearly as good as I wanted them to be. For the past couple of years, I had been struggling with trying to figure out why. With this newfound insight, like the pieces of a quilt or brush strokes on canvas, a picture began to form.

All beings are born with the right to survive, the right to exist and to create their own lives. Each of us has the intrinsic right to be safe, to feel secure and have our basic needs met; things like food, water, and shelter. We also have the right to have our basic emotional needs met; love, acceptance, and nurturing. As a child, I received all of this. My mother and grandparents loved me, fed me, cared for and nurtured me. But, as it does for so many, things happened that caused these basic rights to become skewed. Early childhood abuse by my primary father figure eliminated any sense of safety or security I previously had. His cruel ways and violent temper turned my basic rights into beliefs that because I was born a girl, I was not worthy of existing, that I was "less than" those around, that I had no say in how my body was treated.

Starting when I was about four years old, all I wanted to do was make beautiful things. Sitting in the sunshine, a pie plate full of mud and rocks decorated with flowers held between my hands, I proudly showed my grandmother what I had created. This is one of my favorite childhood memories. The scolding I received for getting dirty, however, is not. And yet, this was how my love affair with creation and expressing my creativity evolved. I would delight in making something, show it off so proudly and then have it dismissed as "cute" or irrelevant. Or worse, I would be punished for making a mess.

As I grew up, life and being creative became more difficult. I would withdraw into my coloring books or embroidery, feeling far safer in the haven of my imagination than in the world of a man who would have screaming, black-eyed rages with little or no provocation. When I did this however, he would make fun of me, telling me to go outside and play with my trucks, not to be "so much of a girl." In truth, being a girl wasn't safe. If I acted like a girl, I was forced to do sexual things that made me feel dirty and ashamed. Yet being a tomboy had its own drawbacks. Tomboys weren't supposed to create beautiful things. They were supposed to be "one of the guys"; strong, dirty and tough. Being soft, gentle, or feminine meant you got hurt, that you were weak, that you were less than. Being tough and hard, with an attitude to match, kept you safe, or at least that's what I thought. But if I acted like a boy, then he wanted to roughhouse and would sit on top of me, pinning my arms down with his knees. He would tickle me until I sobbed, powerless to do anything but beg to be released. I hated every single moment of it. Yet this was also the man that, as a child, I loved and revered above all others.

Gradually, I began to distance myself from my love of creating things. I tried so hard to be who he wanted me to be, but it was impossible. Torn between doing what I loved, and what was safe and expected of me caused a deep rift in my heart. It became so deep I almost couldn't see across it.

It was during that time I became self-destructive. Causing myself physical pain was far easier to deal with than the pain and betrayal I felt in my heart. After a couple of years constantly having to hide self-inflicted cuts and bruises, it all became too cumbersome. I decided there had to be a better way. My creativity began to resurface, with the encouragement of my mom and a couple of dedicated teachers. Writing poetry and short stories became an emotional outlet. Creating pictures with words led to real drawing and then painting. Life was so much better when I was creating.

Of course, with high school and college came boys. Like threads in a tapestry, a pattern developed in my life. As soon as I felt myself getting close to someone, I would break it off and run. No one was going to hurt me the way I had been hurt as a child or make me into something I wasn't.

Then a new person entered my life, one that was far too familiar. His violent temper, so like the black-eyed rages I had grown up with, quickly reduced me to feeling like the terrified child who couldn't say no, who couldn't say stop.

My lifeline was creativity. It made sense to pursue a career that would involve art in some way. So I went to college, and became a graphic designer. With this new guy, creativity once again turned into a target. Everything I made was degraded, dismissed as childish and worthless. I was told to keep it hidden because, "No one wants to see that shit!" Once again, in order to feel safe and secure, I smothered my creativity, denying my deepest yearnings, letting go of the only cord to sanity I had. The few and far between times that it was allowed, creating was reduced to idle play to be indulged only after the chores and housework were done.

Just as it did when I was younger, quenching my creative fire had dire consequences. Depression became a constant companion, filling my days with a tarry blackness that seeped into every crack. In my heart I knew I had a purpose. There had a to be a reason I was alive, there had to be something more to life than what I was living every day. I held on for as long as I could, but slowly my belief in something better died. Any hope I had of making something of myself disappeared. My days grew darker. Severely withdrawn, I rarely spoke to anyone outside of my job. Rejecting my family was easier than the fights that inevitably cropped up every time they came around. The bottom of this black hole appeared on the day I had a vision of killing myself. The vision was so vivid, so real that it shocked me out of my depressed stupor and made me realize that I had to make a change if I was going to survive. On that day I took control of my life and never looked back.

Here and now, all of this began to make sense to me. The sun of my awakening was rising higher, but it wasn't quite at its apex just yet. From the viewpoint of childhood abuse and trauma, my past made a certain amount of sense as far as the reasoning behind the choices I had or had not made. As I looked at my current life through this new lens of *"you have the right to say stop"* some startling things showed up.

Even though I thought I was being strong, being true to

myself, there were still many ways that I was acting like the child who was afraid of being seen. I was afraid of saying or doing the wrong thing. I had created a dual life; spirituality and energetic work in my business, yet I was a completely different person when I was at home. I completely disregarded my spiritual beliefs around my family. It was far easier to ignore who I was than try to explain it to people who may not accept me. Eating foods my body couldn't digest, participating in physical activities that wore me out were all ways I had been saying yes to other people's desires instead of listening to my own inner wisdom. Just as the sun illuminates the shadows, the truth became clearer. On a deeper level, I was still terrified to say stop, to say no, afraid of what the consequences would be.

How could this be true? Years and years of working towards becoming better, stronger, more genuine and I was still afraid to speak up for myself? I was not doing what I desired! Just like that morning in downtown Calgary, cold gray filled my vision and rolled into the core of my being, threatening to take away what I had worked so hard to gain. For a moment, I was consumed with feelings of being a complete failure, an utter fraud. Thankfully, I had come too far to let this derail me. I stood my ground in the swirl of recriminations in my mind, knowing that we are given new levels of understanding only when we are ready for them. This pattern had been revealed so that I could change it, not fall back into it.

The revelation gave me renewed hope, belief that I was moving in the right direction. It explained a lot about the issues

I had been dodging for so many years, it just didn't explain everything. There still had to be more.

I have always been blessed, or cursed, with the need for more. Know more, be more, do more. Thinking about that conversation again, I started digging deeper. There had to be something I was missing. Day after day during meditation or moments of idle thought, I dug and poked, feeling into the nooks and crannies of my soul, the places that didn't really want to be probed. But nothing more came to the surface.

About six weeks after that cold autumn sun was just beginning to rise over Calgary, I sat in my morning meditation. I was stuck and had asked my mentor for help. She gave me one simple task. During my meditation, I asked my heart a single question, "What do you want to tell me?"

Much to my surprise, the answer was immediate. The voice of my heart told me this, "When the man you loved above any and all others in the world sexually abused you, your heart and your trust in the world were shattered. You doubted your heart to tell you the truth because you loved him so much and he betrayed you. That betrayal formed a belief that if you loved something, it would hurt you. You began to distrust your creativity because if you loved to create, then at some point, creating would hurt you. That belief was reinforced each time you were made fun of or punished for creating your art. You also believe that inspiration comes from outside of you, from the Universe, the ultimate source. When you lost your trust in your father, you lost your trust in God. You lost your trust in creative source and how that source speaks to you."

This message was the final piece to the puzzle that I needed to know, the master brush stroke. The sun rose fully on my awakening!

The deeper truths were apparent once I got quiet, gave myself permission, and stopped long enough to look at them. Now I could see how abuse as a child had severely damaged my root beliefs around being "not enough" and "less than." At the point in my life when I was most vulnerable, I had been taught the very essence of my being was bad, and what I desired most in the world was wrong.

Every human being born is creative. Children are insatiably creative. The core of Divine Feminine energy is about creation! To be forced to hide my femininity and deny my creative nature in order to feel safe damaged my sense of self. I had come to believe I had no right to exist, to be loved or be seen for who I was. The pattern developed even further as an adult, with the added belief that my creativity was worthless; my art was something to be indulged only after chores and my job, the "real" work, was done.

It all made so much sense in that moment of clear awareness. No wonder I was denying my creativity, the very essence of my heart and soul. The child within my heart was so afraid of being hurt, of being punished, that she wasn't about to put herself out there any further than she absolutely had to. On the rare occasions that she did, she pulled back in fear of being caught, of being seen, of being called out as a "bad girl" once again.

I had searched for these answers for so many years. I worked so hard to make it all right. Counseling as a child and young adult had proven to be of little help, causing me more confusion. This led to searching for answers outside of the traditional means. I attended metaphysical fairs, received angel readings, connected with groups offering energetic trainings. The new age concepts of energy and spirituality gave me direction to a greater potential, leading me forward like bread crumbs. Meditation, runes, tarot, crystals and stones, I was hungry for anything I could get my hands on to learn, to fill the void inside of me.

Since I was a small child, I had a gift for healing with my hands. At the apex of my creative crisis, after nearly ending my life out of sheer desperation and despair, I switched professional gears and became a massage therapist. More than anything I wanted to help people. I thought this would be the answer I was seeking. This would make me whole and complete. It did prove to be the start of my new beginning. While in massage school, I was introduced to the healing modality of Lomilomi. The indigenous beliefs at the core of this healing practice became my spiritual lifeline. Through lomilomi I met the woman who became my mentor. With her help, encouragement, and an occasional spiritual 2x4 when needed, I dug deeper, went further. I became more than I thought possible. In helping others to heal, I also healed more of myself. When one layer was released, another would always rise to be seen. This was the path I stepped onto when I said yes to healing and it took me to places I never dreamed of. Traveling from the jungles and beaches of Hawai'i all the way up to 17,000 feet in the Andes of Peru, I searched and prayed for answers. The answers were always inside of me, just waiting to be found. Coaching, mentoring, spiritual healing and training, vision quests, and a constant drive to be better than I was the day before led me inward, and upward. It led me to this day.

My journey of healing was like a spiral. I kept returning to the center of my being, each turn of the circle bringing me closer to the truth. It became a whirlpool that pulled me in until I could no longer escape looking directly at what was interfering with my creative heart.

We all have a journey, a path that leads to our deepest inner healing. This inner healing is needed for us to step up and be seen for the magnificent creations that we are. We are all creators, each of us has a creative heart that yearns to be honored, to be heard. When we deny that call, when we smother our natural-born creativity, every part of existence pays the price. Our passion, our creativity, our love is what makes this world go around. Creation is what makes life worth living!

How do we honor this creative heart within us? How do we live our soul's purpose, each and every day? The pieces are all contained here in this book, given to us by each woman who has vulnerably and authentically shared her story. They have given us way points on the map to becoming wholly and purposefully our truest Self! The journey is worth it, my friend. Trust me! You will never be more grateful than the day you say YES to your own heart!

"*I have learned that
when we forget who we are
or stray too far from
our purpose, God will
lead us back to it and in
a way that is uniquely
designed just for you.*"

~unknown

Deborah Finley

Deborah is a practicing Evidential Spiritual Medium, Mentor and Published Author, who has over two decades of experience reading for individuals professionally. She is a Spiritual Teacher, Certified Angel Card Reader and an Ordained Minister.

She has been a Natural Medium all of her life. Since she was a young child, she has had the ability to communicate with spiritual beings, after having a near death experience in December of 1986, her abilities became even more super charged. It is her hope to provide comfort, and a sense of peace to those she reads for, confirming the survival of the soul after our physical death takes place.

In her free time Deborah enjoys painting Angels, and writing. She loves spending time on the beach, with her family at the New Jersey shore and traveling with her loved ones. She is passionate and dedicated to educating, and helping others understand their Gift of Mediumistic abilities.

Email Deborah at mediumdebfinley@gmail.com

Website: www.Angel-Energy.org

Chapter Two

Surrendering to the Divine Plan

Deborah Finley

The Creator, God, has an intelligence far beyond what our human capacity has the ability to conceive or understand.

I was thinking about this, about how we all have those times in life where we think back over our lives, our situations, over the things we have experienced and how we felt. I recalled the very day and exact moment when I realized how important my gift was. I was feeling confused and depressed.

The memories I share are for people like you. Maybe you are struggling? Maybe you don't trust yourself, feel worthy, or maybe you feel like you don't know who you are?

I was born a Natural Medium, so the ability to know and communicate with Spirit has been with me for as long as I can remember.

Everyone has had periods in their life where they have felt

down, right? I know I have, but this time felt different. I just couldn't make any sense out of it. My life was good, and I had every reason to happy, yet every day I was struggling with these relentless thoughts to kill myself! Have you ever felt irrational or crazy? There was no rational reason for feeling like this and yet here I was trying to gather up enough pills to kill myself.

On the day when God reminded me who I was, the thoughts were so bad. I couldn't seem to pull myself together. I was lying in my bed, still in my PJ's when I should have been dressed and on my way already. I had committed to be a parent adviser for a local youth group and had really enjoyed it, up until recently. This was one of those days where everything seemed to be overwhelming. I had a twenty-five-minute drive to get to the meeting. I made myself get up, walked over to the drawer to get clean clothes, thinking the entire time I had to hurry or I was going to be late again. Mindlessly I dressed and threw on my sandals. I went and got the pills, dumped them into my hand and counted them. There were eighty-two. For a brief moment, I stared at them. Carefully I put the pills back into the bottle, picked up the hairbrush, ran it through my hair, and brushed my teeth. I kept looking back at the bottle, so I hid it under the bathroom sink for later.

I felt those now familiar feelings creeping back into my mind. Ignoring them, I put on mascara, some lipstick and pinned my name tag to my shirt. I felt awful. All my thoughts lead back to me hating everything about my life, my appearance, and myself. These days I was always late. I was self-sabotaging.

Those awful thoughts of killing myself were overwhelming. I was confused. I started to feel panicked as I got into my car, hooking the seat belt. I really needed help, and I thought to call a friend.

I remember my whole body was literally shaking as I called her. At first, she didn't answer. I just knew not to leave a message, so I called her right back. When she answered I didn't give her a chance to say anything. I blurted out, "I really need you to do me a huge favor. Please! I need you to fill in for me today as a parent adviser at the school. I'm running so late I'll never make it." There was dead silence at the end of the phone. For a moment I thought she may have hung up. "Hello? Are you there? Hello?" I could barely hear her as she said, "I can't believe you called me just now." I began apologizing to her for waiting until the last minute. She cut me off saying, "No. You don't have to apologize. I will go for you, but afterward, we need to talk. I have a very important question to ask you."

I drove all the way to the school for the meeting and then thought, "The hell with it. I don't want to be here. I just can't do this today," and turned the car around. Driving home, I was contemplating the thoughts I was having, and I found myself saying out loud, "Yep, I'm going to go home right now and kill myself." I had a strange sense of relief after I said this! Weird, right?

I no sooner walked through the door when my phone started ringing. I looked and it was the same friend. I thought, "Oh dear God, the last thing I want to do now is try to explain myself." However, she deserved an explanation, especially after helping me out at the last minute. I felt obligated to repay her with a reading. I knew she desperately wanted one since her child had recently passed away. When I answered the phone, she immediately said to me "Debbie, what made you call me when you did?" I found myself apologizing again adding, "Well I knew you had your federal clearances and would be allowed into the school."

She cut me off before I went on by saying, "No" and emphasizing, "I want to know what it was that made you call me at that EXACT moment?"

Have you ever found yourself telling someone something that you hadn't told anybody? The words just came pouring out of me. I told her I felt myself beginning to panic because I wasn't going to be able to make the meeting on time. She asked me again, "What made you call me at that exact moment?"

I told her my nerves were shot and that I was literally shaking when suddenly she popped into my head, and I called her. I explained that I had been fighting depression and was so confused because I had no reason to be depressed! I added that I thought I was going crazy. "I have to be losing it because I am having these thoughts of killing myself and I have no rational reason to justify why this is happening! I swear to God these thoughts don't make any sense. My life is good! These thoughts feel like they aren't really mine."

I heard a gasp on the other side of the phone, "I just popped into your head?" Her voice reminded me of a wounded child. "Oh my God," she cried, "Debbie, I've been praying for a message, asking God for one to come through to you." I remembered her telling me years ago what I did freaked her out. I heard her say she knew I didn't talk with spirit or give messages anymore and that I had given up reading. She told me that she didn't want to ask me for a message from her child. I felt terrible because I had this ability, a God-given gift, yet I kept pushing away the urge to connect with her child and give her a message.

My friend continued, "Debbie, you said you felt like those thoughts weren't yours." I listened to her intently as she went on to tell me she believed the thoughts were not mine because it was exactly what she was going through and how she had been feeling. I wasn't sure if I heard her right. She said, "Debbie, I didn't want to live anymore." What she said next rendered me speechless. "Today when you called, I was about to swallow a handful of pills that I had been collecting to kill myself." After I heard this admission I felt light-headed, shocked beyond words. Now it was my turn to gasp. She said, "If you hadn't called me at that moment, I would have been dead."

I couldn't find my voice to speak. She was asking me if I thought this could have been her child trying to stop her.

I felt so emotional, my heart was pounding. All I could think of was, "Oh my God!" I didn't tell her about the pills. Wow! Right? I knew this was the greatness of our creator and spirit reaching out through me for the highest good of another and it wasn't just about me.

There it is, the exact moment I knew without any doubt how important my gift was. I now knew what I was supposed to be doing with these abilities. Finally finding my voice, I answered my friend, "Yes, so I called you." I felt my soul purpose ignite and I felt whole once again. In this moment I became aware that I could hear her child clearly and felt the strong presence the spirit close to me. I had a knowing that I was taking on my friends' feelings as my own. I also knew without a doubt that my friends' child was trying to get through to me to help stop her from taking the pills.

Thinking about things afterwards I was left with an understanding that I hadn't been able to figure out while I was experiencing it all. The infinite intelligence of the creator God never ceases to amaze me. It is mind-blowing. I took a moment to experience God's grace, and to thank him. I felt filled with the energy of gratefulness. Deep inside of me, I felt the light of my soul brighten a little more.

Can you imagine if I hadn't called my friend when I did? She would have died, all because I was ashamed of who I was. Thank God on some level, my Soul knew. You know that phrase when someone says, "It isn't all just about you?" It's true. We are all connected in ways we can't even imagine. Our lives are Divinely orchestrated. With this revelation, my mind became clearer and I felt calm, deeply peaceful within of myself.

I have shared this experience with you as a turning point for me personally. The effects of fear had created an illusion that had kept me paralyzed, stuck. The moment I took my power back, the illusions shattered like glass. In a moment's time everything became so clear. I realized I had been living in fear for so long. I had even given up reading because I was so scared and worried about being judged crazy, possibly losing my kids and husband. How ironic that my battle to shut down and ignore these abilities, this gift I was born with, had resulted in so much confusion and negativity.

Clearly, I wasn't able to live fully in the moment. Yes, I was functioning, better than most women even. I am a wife and mother of two children. One of my children was born with a rare syndrome which only one in forty-four million people have. I was a career woman, who was running a successful state-licensed massage school along with working a couple of days at a doctor's office providing rehabilitative and medical-massage. However, because of doubts, superstitions, and other people's belief systems, I found myself fighting a battle within.

I now know the effort it took to ignore and push away what came to me so naturally was an experience I needed on a soul level. Before this experience, I didn't feel worthy and doubted that which was given to me. Do you know what I realized? I realized that what I was doubting was God's intelligence and wisdom. My faith in the creator God was strengthened through this experience. Don't give your power away.

Every experience will mold you into who you are today. My experiences have made me who I am. All of them - the good, the bad, and the ugly. Every single one helping to prepare me to be of service, and to live a purposeful life. I feel truly blessed. Looking back now on this day, I understand how supported I was every step of the way. God and the angels never abandoned me. I was exactly where I was supposed to be, and with perfect timing. This realization freed me from all the doubts and fears I had taken on before my re-awakening. I was no longer conflicted, or afraid to embrace my authentic self. I was no longer defining myself through the opinions of others. Deep inside of me, I felt the light of my soul brighten.

I have learned to value the gifts God gave me without any fears, superstitions, or shame. I pray that you may also see the value in accepting, loving, and embracing your authentic self. Personally, I never want to stop improving on my abilities and learning how to be of better service. I am dedicated to helping others. We are connected, in ways we would never even think about until afterwards. Hindsight is never wrong. Life is nothing short of amazing. I found that I was getting sick all the time, and the doctors couldn't find a reason for it. My mind was filled with anxiety, fear and thoughts of not liking myself much. When I dimmed the light of my soul, little by little, for far too long, what resulted wasn't pretty. It may just be the Creator, his Angels or even an Earth Angel nudging your soul to remember who you are. Let them re-awaken and ignite your soul. It is my hope that by sharing the exact day and moment when I realized how important my gift is, that I have done my part in inspiring you to embrace your authentic self.

Let the light of your soul brighten every day. May you embrace your power, know the potential you have and live your joyful purpose.

"*Those who don't believe in
magic will never find it.*"

~ spoken by Roald Dahl

Brenda Nickolaus

Brenda Nickolaus is a Creativity Empowerment coach, guiding you to live creatively for your well-being! As an empath and highly sensitive being it is important to take care of yourself. She can teach you creative tools to help you feel less stressed and tap into your intuition. Brenda uses a variety of artful tools including nature, intuitive painting, guided meditations, and introduces you to an artful practice. This will help you find clarity, confidence and courage as you navigate your feelings in this world.

As you tap into your creativity through Brenda's coaching in the art of well-being you also connect to your intuition. Using Soul Art and nature helps you explore, finding a more meaningful, creative and joyful magical life in a fun and easy way.

Website: www.brendanickolaus.com

Chapter Three

When the Magic Disappears

Brenda Nickolaus

The day would come unexpectedly when I could no longer connect with the magic of the butterflies dancing among the flowers. No longer would those hours sitting watching the turquoise-colored blue waves inspire me like they had since my first science project in third grade. Where did my sense of awe go when I had connected with the waves at the beach, my favorite place to be? Why was my inspiration gone?

I believe in Magic. It's everywhere! I lived in magic every day of my life as a child. I remember planting a seed in the garden, nurturing it and watching the first sprout magically push through the soil. I was so excited to see it pop up and I imagined the journey it must have been on to be here now.

I know I had a fortunate upbringing, not everyone does. However, I can relate to pain, loss and to healing in order to help others. I was taught that when we look for inspiration in our darkest hours, we really do find it, sometimes through a sequence of circumstances.

I believe we are being guided by angels and spirit to be more open to the magical world around us. We have the best classroom available when we step outside. Nature is here to help us dance, dream, to inspire us and, most of all, to remember kindness and love so we can create and live our best life.

Did you know there is a secret weapon that gets us to open up and talk about our feelings and our lives? I remember how my family went on walks together around the neighborhood, something you don't often see anymore. We would talk about our day, our garden. As we were out pulling the weeds on a warm day and the sweat poured from my brow, what we were really doing was sharing secrets. You know the ones that only best friends might tell each other, or a secret chocolate chip cookie recipe handed down for years that no one was supposed to know about, ever.

The secret weapon is magic, like in our foods. Have you ever picked an apple, peach or strawberries? Take a moment to think about that first sprout, and now you have something to eat. That's magical! I can recall creating delicious meals from the blessings we found in our garden. Perhaps you didn't grow up with a garden, but you can still have an appreciation for the dance of life, the dream, the belief in loving energy that is everywhere in creation. Do you remember a time you took a bite of something and your taste buds came alive?

You thought, "This is the most amazing flavor!" Well, maybe you don't call it magic per se, it sure is magical how everything works in our world and life if we pay attention.

My mom and dad played a huge role in what I believe in today. Dad would always say, "We are from the stars." If you looked up on a bright clear night and saw a crescent moon and perhaps the star of Venus, it would feel magical. Then, when the other twinkling lights appeared, it's like those butterflies or dragonflies dancing through the flowers.

Life reminds me of painting a lotus flower, layers and layers of petals, one over the other, often hiding the original ones on the canvas. We see something and then it disappears. Just like the magician who redirects your attention and suddenly his assistant is gone. My young spirit wanted to know, "Where did the magic go? Would I ever find it again?"

"Those who don't believe in magic will never find it."
spoken by Roald Dahl

I didn't know I would feel so vulnerable sharing this with you. I knew deep inside the signs around me were all connected somehow and someone needed to hear my story. Is it you?

Then the day came when the magic disappeared. I never imagined this could happen.

I felt something deep inside before the call came. I didn't understand the energy I was feeling. I just 'knew' something was wrong. My Dad had been diagnosed with cancer 6 months prior and I had a flight out at the end of the week for another visit. Somehow, I just knew he had passed before the call. The magic disappeared and I didn't know where it went. I was sad, lost and empty. Dad played such a wonderful role in my life, always bringing that sparkle in life to everything, and now it was gone. I felt devastated, sitting in this moment.

One day these feelings would serve me in a way I couldn't imagine. I knew death was a natural thing, but I felt clumsy in the unfamiliar waters of emotions. I wanted to know more about the other side. I had a lot of questions coming up. Of course, there were good days and some days where life takes a turn for the worse. I was in confusion and grief as I was trying to understand it all; life, death and the Spirit world in general.

The relationship of all these synchronous events would lead to a spiritual awakening for me. Soon I would learn how the magic was waiting for me as well.

I was holding in a lot of my grief. Moving on was what was expected I suppose, by others and myself, so I didn't allow myself to feel the pain I was hiding inside. Then the day came when I could no longer continue the facade. My health started taking a turn for the worse. I was suffering from major back pain. Stress just seemed to make it worse.

I remember reading about how your mind, body, and spirit can be out of alignment and that misalignment can cause health issues. I wanted a natural way to deal with the anxiety and negative emotions I was experiencing. I wanted to feel happy again, to find my joy after this long and winding path of grief that was constantly around me. I prayed for guidance and started looking for signs of help. I found it! I had no idea where or how, but it showed up, magically!

As soon as I reached out and asked for help from God, from the universal energies, I felt at peace. My heart felt lighter. Like the parting of clouds on a cloudy day, I could see a light. I started to listen more to the silent nudges of my intuition. I was starting to read and study more about the spirituality of the metaphysical world and started seeing the word Reiki as a healing practice. It said Reiki could bring balance to my life, heal my chakras (energy centers in our bodies) and would fill me with contentment and a sense of deep understanding. I was stepping into the power of co-creating with the universe. Reiki? Is this some sort of magic?

I was curious. No, I was obsessed! I wanted to find out more and understand the Divine synchronicity of events that helped lead me to learn more about Reiki, my life and my purpose.

I listened to my intuition and I followed the trail of bread crumbs I felt spirit was laying out for me. I started paying attention to the little, tantalizing tidbits of information.

Gosh, the memories were flowing and bringing the magic back alive in me, remembering the days I would run barefoot outside and no one worried. My hair would just blow in the wind. Did you ever imagine you were on a spaceship flying out to the stars to explore galaxies when you were on a swing? I was a very imaginative kid obviously. Creativity was a passion that ran deep in me, long before I knew the connection.

I felt things deeply and art journaling helped me connect to my feelings. My mom and dad were always encouraging me to follow my artful heart. One of my favorite childhood memories is sitting outside under my favorite tree smelling the freshly cut grass, with my sketchbook in my lap. Connecting to the sounds of the birds and the beauty around me, I could forget the troubles of the day. I could be lost for hours in drawing when I "saw" something to draw.

Now, as an adult, I picked up my sketchbook once again, sitting out on the back porch drawing angels. I always circled back to creativity and nature for healing my spirit, but I felt I wanted more for my soul healing. I was searching for the magic again. Where was it? Would I ever connect with it again? It is in these moments we make a choice, and I started searching and asking for divine guidance.

One time I was listening to a favorite craft show on TV while I was drawing. I could not believe what I was hearing! One of the ladies mentioned Reiki. She told the host how she saw her angel in a Reiki session and then painted "her" guardian angel. Well, anything with art captured my attention and I wanted to see my angel too! The second sign came when I picked up a Reader's Digest magazine and read an article about a lady experiencing the Reiki circle at her church. She felt the energy as a big hug from spirit and felt loved in the session. Third time's the charm! I read about a Reiki workshop and learning about the attunements at a local metaphysical store. I was hooked!

Life goes on, as it always does. On a very normal workday at home, I received a returned package in the mail. An order from one of my dance photography clients had come back. Having a package returned was quite odd. It had never happened before in all of the mailings I had sent out over the years. I called the lady, apologized, and asked her for the correct address. She responded that the address was correct and she believed in synchronicity. She felt it was a sure sign for us to meet and talk. I was a little thrown off at first. It all seemed more than a little odd but I trusted the synchronicity of the phone call. Surprisingly, I heard the words, "Come on over!" come out of my mouth.

When she arrived and came in the house, I felt like I had known her before. Have you ever had a feeling like this, a déjà vu? She had such a comforting presence. We sat on the sofa in my living room sharing stories. Then I showed her around the house and out into our backyard, where the dog was playing in the sunshine.

As we walked around, she started to share her feelings about my place. She said, "I sense a dog passed away here in this spot."

"Yes!" I exclaimed. One of our dogs had a heart attack a few weeks after my Dad had passed away. I asked her how she knew. She said that she was a Reiki Master and explained she could sense things sometimes, with the help of her connection to spirit. Reiki had helped her tap into the spirit world and sometimes she could talk to spirits and loved ones that had passed on. I sat up and paid attention. I said, "WHAT???" I was so excited! Here is my gift of insight! "Okay," I said. "Have a seat. You must come in and tell me all about it!"

As we talked, she explained that Reiki is a spiritual healing practice. It originated in Japan in the early 20th century and is built on the belief that the body is innately able to heal itself. The word Reiki loosely translates to "universal life energy." This is what I had been looking for. I shared with her all that I had been experiencing. She told me I was awakening to the energy of healing not only for myself but also for guiding others on their path of discovery, to help them lift the layers and see the magic in everyday life.

"And the day came when the risk to remain tight in a bud was more painful than the risk it took to blossom"

~ Anais Nin

During the subsequent Reiki sessions and attunements, I healed and reconnected to the Divine, my higher self and to the magic. By tapping into the Reiki energy, I found I could be creative in my options and how I responded to life's challenges. It helped me transform my grief into messy hands and a happy heart. My creativity grew, and my art started to unfold more and more every day. Experiencing challenges in life is inevitable. I discovered creativity and nature could help me move through life's many layers with grace and ease.

I gained confidence and trust in my intuition and took classes to develop my healing gifts. Experiencing my psychic gifts with more understanding, I was able to connect with my Dad's spirit and many others. It felt so empowering to consciously connect and it created that spark of curiosity in my life again.

I learned how Spirit can guide us and take many forms. Have you ever felt a heavenly presence? My favorite memory is of an angel with a horse!

One evening I took a long walk, not really paying attention to where I was going. It had been a super stressful day and I felt the heaviness of every footstep. When I finally looked up, I realized I had taken a different path than normal and somehow ended up at a stable. I could smell that distinct scent of horses. A lady was there by the fence, a beautiful horse in the pasture just on the other side. For a moment, everything seemed to stand still. We started to talk and she reached out with the most gentle touch, giving me a hug, telling me it would be alright. I said

I was fine and then started crying. She offered words of love and encouragement. I felt an overwhelming sense of calm and stood there transfixed; being present in the moment, listening to the sounds of nature, feeling the warmth of the horse under my hand. I felt so much better and calmer as I walked home.

Later I went back to thank her but as I pulled in the driveway of the stables, the place looked deserted. There was a small trailer off to the side. I was so confused. Getting out of my car, I went and knocked on the door. I inquired about the lady with the horse and was told no one had been on the property for a long time. Had this been a visit from an angel? I think so! We have to believe in the magic to see it. I often think back to that magical experience and realize how she empowered me to know that I would be okay.

"If you knew what unseen forces are at work on your behalf at all times, you would be dancing in the streets."

~ Abraham

Reiki was now part of my healing journey. I would sit outside in the backyard with my sketchbook in my lap, connecting again to the inner child of long ago that knew, and remembered the magic. It was time to explore and reconnect with the spirit of nature. Everything seemed more vivid and alive, from the bright yellow on the flowers blooming in my garden to the intense greens in the leaves blowing in the wind.

I am so happy I trusted and followed my Divine guidance; one of the things my Dad told me, "Trust your gut feelings!" Through divine synchronicity, I found the magic again. I discovered the healing power of Reiki, and the alchemy of how art and nature help heal our soul.

I discovered how to expand my own awareness and consciousness from these teachings. They helped me connect with my unique inner spiritual soul source so I could live with calmness and joy, even in the tough times. Following the Reiki Precepts enabled me to savor the joys of life and helped me in the bittersweet time I was caring for my husband. During his time with cancer we tapped into the healing energy and were able to have more time together than what was predicted. I understood the grief process, being fully present for him during his treatments and for my children when it came time for him to cross over. I held him as long as I could and now, I will hold on tight to the love we shared.

Reiki was now a container for me to understand and to believe that there is hope when we lose someone. We can find the magic again as we are shuffling through the many layers of life. I could see the grief was lifting. It reminded me of a feather; light, swirling and floating up through the air.

As I remember all the truly divine synchronicities that have helped me soar and rise above the obstacles in my life, I feel empowered. I feel motivated to move through experiences and be present as life shifts. As I guided others through Reiki sessions and attunements, I was able to share my creativity and encourage others to take a creative first step to a better life. Encouraging them to find the magic. Yes! It was back, and we can always find it again if it disappears.

It's been over 20 years since I first learned about this healing modality. There have been so many changes that have taken place in my life path over the years. Now I can connect the dots and feel the pull on the lifelines like a spider web, connecting all that is. I can feel how it put me on the spiritual path that leads me to seeing the joy, the fun and the meaning of life on my creative vision quest of healing. Believing in magic is the way. Moving forward in my life as a Reiki master, I want to continue sharing this healing with others. Sharing Reiki makes me feel excited when I am coaching others to explore their creative side and see them step into the healing flow.

Connection to the spiritual world has strengthened my creative spirit. I was transformed through soul art consciousness. It has changed me so much, to my very core. I love the journey it has taken me on. Remember this "You are allowed to be both a masterpiece and a work in progress at the same time."

That first step is the choice that will change your life. Everything in my life has become so much more sacred. It helped awaken my power to bring joy and a healing magical artful vision to the world. I believe we are all creative and our souls long to find an outlet. We need to create the free time we had as children to explore and just do it. As we reach deep into ourselves, we find the little one again, the one that believed in magic. Give her a hug and invite her to come out and play!

"Never lose your sense of wonder. Art has the power to transform, to illuminate, to educate, inspire and motivate."

~ Brenda Nickolaus

*"You'll see it
when you
believe it."*

~ Wayne Dyer

Nanette Nuvolone

A certified "Heal Your Life" Workshop Facilitator and Coach, Nanette holds a Bachelor of Arts in Psychology. Her mission to raise her own consciousness led Nanette to the philosophies of Louise Hay ten years ago. It was her discovery of Hay's transformational book *"You Can Heal Your Life"* that inspired her to discard old belief systems and heal aspects of her life that no longer served a purpose.

Nanette feels "truly blessed" to be able to inspire others along their spiritual journey to create the lives they truly desire through her workshops and one on one coaching.

womanilluminated@gmail.com

Website: www.illuminatingthechaos.com

Chapter Four

You Can Heal Your Life

Nanette Nuvolone

I was sitting alone one day at a Perkins Pancake house. I had just finished chowing down on a Belgian waffle. You know the ones with the big, fat, deep pockets that fill up with syrup that oozes out of every crevice. As I lamented over my poor choice for breakfast and was growing impatient waiting for the waitress to come with my check, I felt an odd sensation behind my left knee. That was strange, I thought. However, before I could investigate what was causing the feeling, the waitress appeared with check in hand and I was on my way. I paid my bill, grabbed one of those complimentary mints and quickly went out the door.

As I got to my car, my intuition and curiosity kicked in and guided me to investigate the annoyance I had felt. I lifted my left pant leg and let out a gut-wrenching scream! There on my leg was an ugly spidery thing, a tick that had lodged itself into my leg. Without thinking, I instantly grabbed a hold of it and pulled it off my leg. I figured I had removed countless numbers of ticks from my cats, so this was easy and there wasn't anything to be concerned about. Having just returned from Florida where I had spent the last month dealing with the sudden death of my father, I figured I was already in enough pain. I refused to have any more so I didn't even bother going to the emergency room.

Once home, my intuition was still nudging at me, making me uncomfortable. I had an idea. "I know," I thought, "I will consult my pendulum!" It seemed like a practical decision, don't you think? My eyes moved back and forth with the motion of the swinging crystal as I considered which signal would tell me the best decision. A front to back motion would be my signal to go to the ER, while a left to right motion meant stay home. It may sound silly to some, but I counted on it to give me the guidance I needed. Well the stupid thing stayed completely still. Imagine that? "Well, damn!" I thought. "Now I have to go consult the heavy artillery." I pulled out my *"Archangel Raphael Healing"* oracle deck. Archangel Raphael would surely tell me what to do. I held the cards in my hands, shaking a bit, feeling the glossy paper, looking at the beautiful archangel graphics and shuffled away, believing the message would be absolutely what I needed to do. I scanned the cards, felt for the 'very' best one and turned it over. "Listen to your intuitive feelings". Seriously? Geez, if I could clearly hear my intuition, I wouldn't be asking these damn cards! The more nervous I got, the more cards I chose, clouding my intuition even further.

I didn't know what the hell to do, so I grabbed a plastic baggie, placed the blood sucker inside, and took off for the ER.

As I sat in the ER waiting area, I realized I didn't know anything about Lyme disease. Really I didn't think I had anything to worry about yet I found my mind plagued by thoughts of the disease. The nurse grabbed the little plastic bag with that tiny blood sucking ninja in it. She didn't seem too concerned. I felt better when she told me that it hadn't been feasting on me for too long since it wasn't engorged or filled with my blood. On brief examination, the main indicator - a pinkish red bulls eye rash - was not found. That was a good sign too. She took extra care to make sure none of the tick's body parts were left in my leg, just in case. She grabbed her surgical knife, scraping away at my leg where the little bugger had ambushed me and then sent me on my way. There was no prescription for antibiotics, so I guessed that's good. They didn't schedule a follow up appointment either so I thought, "No worries."

Off I went as if it were any other day, even though I was more than a bit shaken by the whole experience. Because of how I was feeling I did the next logical thing. I headed to the grocery store to buy a package of E.L. Fudge cookies. They always seemed to help relieve my anxiety. I sat in the parking lot of the Wegmans grocery store until every morsel, every smooth lick of fudge had been devoured. Now I felt okay. Besides, who has time for the possibility of a tick-borne disease when I was so overcome with grief.

Naturally I was feeling sad that my dad was dead. I was also feeling incredibly guilty. I hadn't answered the phone when he had called just a few days prior to Christmas. Sitting with the phone in my hand, I saw the number flash across the screen and listened to it ring while debating whether I should answer it or not before letting it go to voice mail. This may sound insensitive. However, Dad was always asking me for money for his terrible heroin addiction. "Maybe," I thought, "he could just be calling to wish me a Merry Christmas. That would be logical and welcomed." Yet there was still a part of me that felt like there was an ulterior motive as usual. Once the voice mail came in, I decided to listen it. Tears flowed down my cheeks as I heard him, for what would be the last time, wish me a Merry Christmas and say, "I love you." I intended to call him back but for whatever reason I hesitated. Needless to say, I had been replaying his last message again and again.

It was Christmas night around 11:00 PM when the call came in. My dad had been rushed to the hospital. I was numb with shock and disbelief. After hanging up, I cried until I was exhausted then feel asleep. The loud ring of the phone woke me abruptly from my sleep at 3:45 AM. Answering it, I heard those dreaded words, "I'm sorry. Your father is gone." The intense pain of absolutely unbearable guilt ran through my veins. Simultaneously I felt sick, sad and depressed. I felt as if I was hooked up to a torture machine, like the one in the movie "The Princess Bride" that was in the Pit of Despair. If you've ever watched the movie, Prince Humperdinck sets the machine to the highest level possible that sends Westley into a catatonic state resembling death. His squeals of agony reverberated throughout the forest. Just like Westley, my body shook uncontrollably. I cried, pleading with God for this to be a mistake. If only I could go back to that day, pick up the phone and tell Dad I loved him too, maybe this would all be different today and I wouldn't feel so guilty. Perhaps the pain of the tick was there to remind me of the pain of my guilt when it decided to infiltrate my blood. Was this a coincidence, a message or a punishment?

The days and nights would slip into each other as my remorse grew and the physical pain escalated. The left side of my face was now numb and I had no control of the entire left side of my body. I began fumbling as I walked, wobbling like a toddler trying to take their first steps. It was time to make an appointment with the doctor.

A few days later my worst fears were confirmed, I had Lyme. No!! The pain had become so intense I would sit up against a wall and push my head into it, hoping the pressure would counteract the pain. Occasionally, I would find relief but most other times I just felt defeated, crying myself to sleep. I felt so angry, so alone. None of the protocols the doctors prescribed worked. Praying I would die, I began to slip into a dark hole of depression.

I started researching how people could jump from a tall bridge to commit suicide. While driving I would look at the bridges thinking, "Would this one be a worthy contender for the demise of my final day?" I frequently drove over the Driscoll Bridge in New Jersey. It is a very tall bridge and I would always contemplate if jumping off this bridge could be the solution, the end to my pain. "Just jump Nanette!" With my luck, I would probably survive. The suicidal thoughts were now predominant in my mind. I berated myself constantly and felt God was punishing me. I knew I wanted to end my life, I couldn't go on. I had to find a way to leave my body, to be rid of this crippling pain.

Prior to all this I had spent time studying the creative power of the mind. One day I had a thought. What if I started to focus on my heart every night, to stop it from beating? Would this work? As I laid my head down on the pillow that night, with tears streaming down my face, I began to visualize my heart losing its ability to pump fresh oxygen rich blood to my lungs. My belief was so powerful, I had no doubt my mind could and would change the physiology of my body.

Now you may be thinking, "Nanette, why didn't you just use your focus for healing?" It was Louise Hay, author of the transformational book, *"You Can Heal Your Life"*, that introduced me to this concept many years ago. However, I was so far down the rabbit hole, I was unable to fathom that healing was even possible at this point and my faith was non-existent. The mindset of someone in great pain is to seek instant relief when they feel hopeless. The most viable option at that time for me was death. I had far more belief in my ability to facilitate my own demise than I did my recovery.

Every night before I would doze off to sleep, I set an intention. Feeling the immense amount of grief and negativity I was storing in my heart I focused on my intention and commanded my heart to stop. Tears streaming down my face, I'd visualize it turning black and losing its ability to pump fresh, oxygen-rich blood to my lungs.

Much to my dismay, the next morning would come, and I'd still be here. I was convinced that God wouldn't let me die and that I was destined to suffer! This behavior went on for some time, as I grew relentlessly bitter and more angry at God. Have you ever felt denied your own divinity in life? I was miserable, and mad.

Finally, I knew that I had to make a decision. The day came when I was able to escape the prison of depression long enough to get myself to a new alternative doctor. She ran a series of traditional and energetic tests on me. As she looked at the results, she noticed an interesting correlation with the energy of my heart. The doctor showed me, curious about what was causing this strange reading. I felt like I had been punched in the stomach. Crying, I told her I didn't want to live anymore. I had decided against taking my own life and came to see her instead. I expressed to her how I felt I had the power to stop my heart from beating with my own thoughts. The tests result in her hand confirmed what I was doing was actually working.

It was astonishing. I had two simultaneous reactions to this news. One was joy because I thought, "Oh my God, it's working. Look how powerful I am!" And the other was pure despair, "Oh my god, it's working. I am purposely influencing an internal organ to function poorly." Now what? What choice would I make ?

I knew something had to change! In that moment I knew 'I' had to change. The pain of staying the same became stronger than the pain of changing. Faith in my healing had previously eluded me and using God as a scapegoat had become my coping mechanism. I was the one stuffing my grief and turning it into pain. It wasn't God causing my pain. I had deliberately put myself in a prison, while I was holding the keys the whole time. Have you ever felt like you were locked in a prison, your freedom stripped from you? That is the experience of a person who has given her power away, and even giving away your power shows you how powerful you are.

Little by little I started to change my behavior. Instead of praying to die before I went to bed, I would set the intention to wake up with joy, having faith that I'd be guided in how to create those experiences the following morning.

The first day when I woke up, I wasn't suddenly transformed into a giddy teenager who had just met Justin Bieber. Instead of feeling amazing, I felt dismal and depressed.

All I wanted to do was break down and cry. It took me a few moments to realize this was what I trained myself to do for the past few months. I had conditioned my body to become my mind. If I seriously wanted to break the habit of being a woman who woke up emotionally tormented, I needed to create new patterns that would override the cycle of negativity.

The next morning, I brought out the heavy artillery. Dancing to Led Zeppelin, Pit Bull and Van Halen each morning became my greatest pattern interrupter. Those bands turned into my new best friends. My life was like a scene in "Groundhog Day" and I was Bill Murray, finally ready to stop repeating and reliving the same day over and over again.

Now it was time to get brutally honest. Every time I listened to the last message my father left on my cell phone before he died, I was torturing myself. I prayed to heal the self-inflicted guilt, to receive an answer. Almost immediately I dropped my old flip-style cell phone. It hit the concrete so hard it shattered. When I bent down to pick it up, it was barely held together by one flimsy wire. I cradled it in my hands and frantically thought, "Oh no! What have I done?" Driving to the phone store, I prayed nervously they could salvage it. They had to fix it or what would I do? After the phone dealer examined my poor, shattered phone they told me it was beyond repair and had to be replaced. I was devastated. Those precious last words, "I love you," were gone forever except in my heart and memory.

Sometimes we have to let go of what's killing us, even if it's killing us to let go. Letting go in this moment meant I would never hear my father's voice again. I had to seriously ask myself, "If I want to heal, are my actions truly in alignment with the outcome that I have been praying for?" And if not, was I willing to surrender what was getting in the way of my healing?

I made a decision on that day and claimed, "I am ready!" The first thing I knew I had to release was guilt. Continually berating myself for something that happened in the past was pointless. I am here to tell you guilt will never make you feel better. I had to let go of punishing myself for something I simply could not change.

The second thing I realized was I had to find a state of peace. My own personal peace could only begin with compassion for myself. It was important for me to acknowledge that I was doing my best in the moment. I also asked myself, "Would I forgive someone else for the same actions?" If a friend shared the same story with me that I just shared with you, I would have compassion for her.

Next, I had to dig deep to cultivate compassion for my father. He had many struggles to endure and the truth was, I really didn't know his story. While I had accepted him for who he was, I realized there was still that little girl inside of me that just wanted her daddy to call her because he loved her.

Research published by the National Center for Biotechnology Information demonstrated that the practice of forgiveness helped diminish feelings of guilt over time.

If you relate to this and truly want to heal, ask yourself, "What step will I take to free myself from this guilt?"

I found that forgiveness exercises helped me. I actually do them in a mirror. Place your hand on your heart, look into your own eyes and say, "I am willing to forgive you". It may feel uncomfortable at first, just continue with this statement. Use it as frequently as needed or whenever you feel guilt arise. Eventually you will easily say, "I forgive myself for _____ and I set myself free."

Using this process consistently has helped me forgive my father. I realized I was only hurting myself by harboring resentment toward him and allowing myself to re-experience those emotions every day. I had to forgive him and forgiving him meant letting it go and no longer bringing that scenario into my current awareness. I was ready to do whatever it took to start healing.

Is there someone you need to forgive? Think about that person. Is it someone from your past? Is it someone in the present? How do you feel when you think of them? Think of that person and write down a list of ten positive aspects about them. If you can only come up with one, start there. Then use the forgiveness practice from above, starting with "I am willing to forgive you." Work with that phrase for as long as you need until you can easily say, "I forgive you for _____ and I set you free." I've used this process with much success for many situations in addition to forgiving my father.

Another step in my healing process was cultivating a gratitude practice. I had not been feeling particularly grateful for Lyme Disease and I certainly didn't have an attitude of gratitude about my father passing away. Nonetheless, I knew that taking my focus off what I viewed as negative and focusing on something positive would put me in a much better space for healing.

When you're sitting in negativity, you are saying "yes" to it. Whenever you're in a negative state, negativity is active in your vibration, and the momentum will continue in that direction. It's why, when you wake up in the morning and say, "UGH, today's gonna be a bad day," guess what, YOU'RE RIGHT.

I knew the antidote was gratitude, but at that time I was so low on the emotional scale, I couldn't just jump up to a higher vibration. I had to start by slowing down the momentum of what I didn't want. To do this I began opening up to the possibility that there was the potential to find a better feeling.

In that place of potential, focus on what you DO want. Allow the possibility of what you want to raise your vibration. When you sit in a vibration that is higher, you will experience it. Say "yes" to being open to possibilities and you will feel better.

If you are having challenges finding something to be grateful for, look around you and borrow someone else's gratitude. What do I mean by that?

One day my friend called me and had just experienced an answered prayer that filled her with gratitude. While I couldn't quite conjure up my own feeling of gratitude, (remember, it's the feeling that elevates you) I could open myself to the feeling of gratitude she was experiencing. I imagined how open her heart was, how grateful she was feeling for her answered prayer. I was able to close my eyes, step out of my own scenario for a moment and walk myself through her experience, knowing that if I could borrow her feeling of gratitude, I could activate the energy of gratitude in myself.

And that's the key right there. She created an attitude of gratitude that resulted in an answered prayer. Her experience reminded me I could create that too. I felt gratitude for my friend's experience - because I knew that the creator of all that is resides in me, as much as it resides in her; as much as it resides in each of you. In those moments when you can't muster it up for yourself, step into the gratitude that someone else is experiencing. In spiritual truth, we are all connected, and all have the power of creation. The good that someone else has created, is also possible for you to create.

I hope that you will reflect upon your life and if my story resonates with you in any way, please make a decision to use your power to heal your life too.

"*The wild woman
never fades;
she is constantly
shaking loose everything
that is not pure soul.*"

~ Shikoba

Bonnie Bonadeo

Bonnie is known as The Connection Coach plus Founder of The Beauty Agent Network Speaker–Educator Resource, The Education Agents, and BonnieBonadeo.com—Coach & Speaker, Syndicated Host, Audio Influencer and International Best-Selling Author.

A beauty and wellness industry professional with over 25 years of experience, she has mastered many levels and achievements. As a 2013 Enterprising Women and 2016 Cover of Salon Today Coaches Guide, she is a Certified Emotional Intelligent Speaker, Executive Business Coach, 5x International Best-selling Author of "Success in Beauty" and "Empowering You and Transforming Lives," The Power of 50, Experts and Influencers; The Leadership Edition, plus a syndicated Radio Host, podcaster, and audio influencer to over 50,000 listeners monthly on BEaUty Inside and Out Show and BEaUtiful Brans Inside and Out.

Bonnie speaks authentically on her struggles and successes as a person, leader, speaker, and entrepreneur to foster growth and awareness in others. She is the essence of being the beauty agent and of her brand which is all about Connecting You to You!

Bonnie@BonnieBonadeo.com
www.BonnieBonadeo.com

Chapter Five

Spirit is (supposed to be) Shaky?

Bonnie Bonadeo

There was this moment in my life when I was forced to succumb to changes, wanted or not. In this moment, there was a form of resistance that stepped in, and in my case, it was massive. It showed up as a fighter with serious anger issues. I was not the weepy, middle-aged woman leaning on her friends for support. I withdrew and became angry with the world, because of course, the world was to blame, right?

Well, the world was not to blame. I had to take some serious ownership of my life, past and present, to have the future I desired and dreamed of. I discovered ownership was easy to say but much more difficult to grasp and comprehend when you cannot get out of your own way. I was willing to be more than a victim in life and I knew I wanted to be the student as well. You know the adage, "When the student is ready, the teacher will appear." Sometimes in life we are surprised by who or what the teacher shows up as. Certainly, I was not prepared for the many teachers that showed up for me.

Fighting this fighter/victim-in-disguise mentality I learned that as humans, we are defined as emotional beings first, then logical beings second. We feel before we think. Our body responds to stimuli first and our thoughts analyze the process. It is all very much how we are hard wired to survive. The survival mode states this choice for us to determine an action: ARE WE IN DANGER? or ARE WE SAFE? Now for those of you that are half-full folks, you can turn it around, but the truth is the brain determines DANGER over SAFETY first. It does not have the capacity to know or distinguish between perceived danger or real danger. It just forces you to prepare for danger and then act when something does not feel right. And nothing felt right in my life, so I was in a constant state of danger, perceived and real!

Back to the adage, "When the student is ready the teacher appears." The teacher may be disguised as a real teacher, another person who enters your life and teaches you something, like mathematical equations or how to post an image on Instagram or other logical ways we learn. I will reference this as logical or neocortex learning.

However, the real learning we must be prepared for and accept in life is emotional learning. The accident, the betrayal, the tragedy, the death, the divorce, the stuck-ness, the doubt, the insecurities that appear to have no basis for existing, the past trauma that we have not healed properly and keeps reoccurring in our life. This type of learning is based in the emotional part of the brain, or the limbic system, and it will always come from memories, experiences, survival and the need to feel safe. Once I learned this, as a logical person I was able to view my actions and start to see some patterns of self-destruction and self-sabotage.

I understood emotional learning can start very early. In some research, it can start in past lives, the womb and of course early childhood. I categorized this as "I can't explain how I know, or it falls into what I don't know and can't figure out for myself." This is my story, the "how did I get to 40 years old with so much going for me including a very happy and solid upbringing, only to have it all start to breakdown as if it was a planned that way?"

It started with me being the 3rd girl in my family. Somehow I knew as a baby that my father wanted a boy, that I should have been a boy. It progressed through my childhood of being a tom boy, very athletic and desiring to grow up and be an astronaut or lawyer, very male dominated positions in the 70's. It seemed simple enough. As a girl I wanted more out of my life than to be a stay at home mom. Not knocking that, my mom was a stay at home mom. But I knew our generation was going to be different. I saw women taking giant leaps. As a child, I knew from my "valedictorian style" kindergarten graduation speech when I stated, "I am going to grow up, work hard like my daddy and carry a briefcase," that dream was going to be fulfilled no matter what.

Although I had many successes in my early 20's and 30's,

it was at age 40 that my world started to spin out of control. Illness, divorce, hair loss, home loss, friend loss, love loss. It was like I was viewed as the monster from the black lagoon. Some of these changes were by choice, but I was not prepared for the swell and the further fall-out that ensued. Of course, like anyone when their world is falling apart, I sought help like therapy, from traditional to non-traditional approaches. Yes, some of it worked and some of it didn't. Regardless, I had to get to the bottom of why I wasn't working anymore.

As divine intervention would happen, a friend asked me to attend an event on emotional intelligence. To support her, and to help me overcome my recluse behavior, I reluctantly accepted her invitation. I was not prepared for the absolute connection that occurred for me when I felt like I witnessed a rope of some sort connecting me to this content and to this teacher.

I knew I needed to know more, and this was the person that was going to help me. This was the beginning of my transformation, personally and professionally.

It started with a coaching session. Three very important questions were presented to me:
1. What is the reason you are so angry?
2. What could you be doing with your time and energy if you weren't so angry?
3. Who could you be if you were not angry all the time?

Somehow, these questions brought me to my knees but with full on resistance; I AM NOT ANGRY! I'M DOING FINE, THIS IS HOW I AM! Yet, number three hit home. I could see and hear my anger. Thinking, "Could I actually be someone who is not angry?" I was forced to think deeper. "WHY AM I ANGRY AT ALL?" I have a fantastic life and upbringing. I had no real answers that didn't start with excuses and me feeling like a fighting victim.

As I progressed through coaching, I started to learn more of the brain science, which helped me see the very logical aspects of how we as humans have developed over millions of years. I found this fascinating and became inquisitive to this non spiritual arena. Although there is plenty of research, to this day we are still unsure exactly how the brain functions. In the end, it provided me insight on patterns that were becoming apparent to the unraveling of my life. This pattern, if you hit the rewind button, showcased a series of stories that started from a very young age, even womb stage, of my life. Each chapter ended with a layer of armor I had put on to protect myself. Eventually the armor would become too heavy for me to bear any longer.

Even though this very neuro-driven information became my hero and savior, looking back into my past, the connection that was showing up had a very interesting divine and spiritual foundation to it. Which, by the way, confused the hell out of me in my journey. Is this science or spirituality? There was not one connection in finding my authentic self that did not include an unexplainable divine path.

In Eckhart Tolle's book, "*A New Earth*", there is a chapter on illusion. The first three times I read it, it didn't make much sense. So, I found a teacher and coach on this concept, and learned how to understand and apply his teachings. As a very young child, I created a story. We will call it, "I was not wanted." This became the original illusion that fiercely propelled me forward, establishing this identity of myself that would forever be instilled within me unknowingly. Living my life within this belief of "I am not wanted" caused me to do everything in my power to be wanted.

My anger showed up because there were parts of my life that I had not healed including a deep-seeded fear that I was not safe and I was not wanted. I didn't know this was my story, it had formed at such a very young age. Yet it became my entire belief system of protecting myself. The more I protected myself, the more unsafe I became.

I was sexually assaulted at five by a neighborhood pedophile. That formed a strong message that being a girl is very unsafe and a vulnerable gender in the world. By the time I reached high school, I was lost, angry and felt cheated that, as a woman, I did not have the same opportunities available to me in life as men. This was not a sexual identity issue for me. I was very much a girl in life, but I felt very uncomfortable in my own skin, partly because of my early beliefs of "I am not wanted" and "It's not safe to be a girl!"

Owing to the fact I was a girl (an angry girl) and also failing high school, I was given a few choices to make school work. My counselor offered two possible directions in order for me to graduate. They were agriculture and cosmetology. I reduced my expectations in life and went into beauty school. By the time I was eighteen I had graduated and was working in the beauty industry. I found I was creative, which gave me an outlet. My personal drive started to form around how I could find success in the business side of this industry which, believe it or not, was highly male-dominated. Over several years in my career, I mastered many positions of leadership and started to really find my outer strength. I found myself running around the world with a briefcase and the feeling that I, as a woman, was breaking through glass ceilings and achieving success.

Then the infamous biological clock started ticking. Well, going off like a fire alarm actually. Being a busy, successful career woman, I always believed I would have children one day. Now that "one day" was looming. After more than a year of trying, traveling and tribulations, I asked the question again, "Why is this not working? Why am I not working?" Again, the intersection of logic and spirit opened its door for me and another friend invited me to a seminar. The woman shared a story of how she could not get pregnant, and yet had a child. There I was, wondering, "Is my whole life planned out to attend seminars and get a divine message?"

I met with the doctor she referred me to, who again had a very powerful question for me. "Do you want to know why you can't get pregnant or do you want to have a baby?" Pretty clear the latter was the answer. Within 24 hours I was on my fertility journey and pregnant within 4 weeks. Now at this point, the clarity of my desires and the ability to manifest them had me feeling like superwoman. Could I really be this powerful? Or was there a guide guiding me through life? My faith and belief were still shaky. Personal power or spirit was up for debate. I knew my life was about to change. In this moment, of now knowing I was pregnant, but also (intuitively) knowing it was going to be a boy, I had to own the fact that I would be the mother of a son. I would be gifted and tasked to raise a man in the world. This should be interesting.

It turned out to be a difficult pregnancy and delivery. I cursed the males in my life for such struggles. Yet there he was, this perfect little man, who had chosen me as his mother. Again the questions, "Did he choose me by faith? Spirit? Or was it just simple human evolution?" Knowing I had to balance being a career woman and now a mom, I needed to get back in the world, working and finding my place in it. Once my son turned four, I was a divorced and single mom.

This new life forced me to seek more freedom, financial and autonomous. This led me to starting my own business, once more taking flight into another transformational journey. I discovered I was not recession proof, losing everything material including my home. Financial devastation and outright failing as an entrepreneur, I was devastated I was failing in life. "My intention was good but did my timing suck?" was the question I kept asking myself. Once again, the connection of a friend and yet another seminar drove me into the abyss of my inner self, questioning everything I had known and everyone I trusted including myself. How much deeper did I have to go? When was this self-reflection going to stop? How many more layers must I peel back to get to the real me, the person I am supposed to be inside and out?

My struggles were not only real emotionally, now they were showing up physically. I was in pain, real pain, yet no doctor could get to the bottom of my pain other than to say, "You seemed stressed." For fuck sake, "Yes! I am stressed. Help me! Help me figure my life out!" It went beyond being medicated for a short time. I truly had to surrender this shaky life, pull up my big-girl panties and suck it up. I did this by doing the deeper work with another coach. I allowed myself to hang out in the corner of my family room, in the corner of my couch, in the corner of my little nondescript world, for an entire year. Yes, I still had to be a mom, show up for work and such. My surrender became me being very still and going within and actually feeling stuff. Stuff I had suppressed for years, stuff I had tried to hide with being a driven, confident, strong leader. Which, in reality, was fearful, insecure and "don't let them see you sweat" all based on not feeling wanted. The story unfolds, and I finally get that transformation. Finding my authenticity is based in the following;

Forgiveness: Not forgiving others caused me harm throughout my life. Although highly recommended, truly forgiving myself for making the best choices with what I had at

69

the time and knowing there is nothing to forgive to begin with and that it is just a life of experiences.

Acceptance: Truly accepting my life for all its love, glory, hardship and crap, and trusting that it is designed by spirit.

Surrender: Not waving the white flag but the natural response of acceptance that there is no battle to battle. My battle was the original illusion of the story I crafted when I did not have the proper tools to protect myself. In the end I don't need protecting to live, I am living in the present.

Ownership: Really authentically owning my life, my mistakes, and my successes. And here comes the twist. There is no need to remove or fix the original illusion as it was my gift. Not being wanted allowed me to participate, collaborate and connect with others so fearlessly that I am a contribution to humanity.

The ultimate learning from my teacher over time was this - we all have a story and it is worth sharing at any cost, as you never know who may need to hear it. A story has 2 parts:

1.   The factual experience that happened
2.   The meaning you give it

I can forgive, accept, surrender and own all the factual experiences that have happened in my life. However, the meaning I gave to my story happened at a very young age, by a five-year-old Bonnie who did not have the mental capacity to logically protect herself. So today, I get to rewrite the meaning my story represents. I get to share the journey in full, including the successes of how my gift of "not being wanted" gave me the life I have today.

I did the work; I felt the pain to get to the joy. I am forever grateful for gaining trust most of all. Trust in others, trust in the process, trust in men and most importantly, trust in me. I look at the world with wonder and curiosity. I look deeper into people's challenges, but not with impatience and judgement like before because of my own insecurities. Now I look with compassion, and understanding that we cannot know what other people may be feeling unless we know their experiences or have walked in their shoes for even a day. I trust my intuition, my divine journeys and my future.

Today, my life is extraordinary! I found the dream. My business life is filled with joy through my work as a speaker, coach, author and podcaster, sharing my stories in life and giving space for others to share their stories. The work I love supports others in finding their authentic story, uncovering what is holding them back or keeping them stuck while being courageous enough to declare, "We deserve a life we love!" I love my personal life with my fiancé, (yes, 3rd time is a charm. Or is it divine intervention? That's another story to be told.) I love my friends, my family, my son who is such an amazing spirit and contribution to this world. I can see his future with pride as he enters into the work force as a smart and compassionate young man. All my experiences, good and bad, have shaped my life and filled my heart with passion to be a better and brighter spirit, but also allow my human to shine.

My scars were witnessed, the pain no longer exists but the memory is present to own my fate, my being, and my humanness. It's my life, it's me. I'm Bonnie and I have the strength to accept that Spirit is supposed to be a little shaky!

"*She was swimming
in a sea of other people's
expectations,
women had drowned
in seas like that.*"

~ Robert Johnson

Jenny Pederson

Jenny Pederson is a life coach and motivational speaker for women and teens who desperately want to say "screw it" to mediocrity, and live full out once and for all!!! Through her in-your-face jokester personality, workshops, and life changing coaching programs, she is here to help you tap into your unique personality to create a kickass career, a happy family, and the time/money freedom to live the life you want… NOW!!!

In her free time, you can find the crazy mom in the stands at her kid's sports events (or coaching them), hosting the biggest, baddest shindigs in the neighborhood, or lounging by a campfire in the woods.

www.jennypederson.com

Chapter Six

Not Your Mother's Guide to Supermom

Jenny Pederson

It was a cold Friday night in December as I paced my living room, nervously waiting for my roommate to get back from Walmart. Why did I have to open my big mouth? Why couldn't I have just gone to the party and not drank alcohol? Yeah right, I was the loud friend, the competitive drinker, of course they would be suspicious. Instead, I had to tell my roommates there was a possibility that I was pregnant and that I probably shouldn't go partying with them that night. I was too chicken shit to even go to the store and buy a damn test. What a great mom I'm going to be.

The door flew open as they got back with the test. I locked myself in the bathroom while my roommates waited patiently outside. I hated that they knew, but there was no hiding it now. If I was pregnant the whole world was gonna find out about it! I felt so ashamed and embarrassed, but I was glad that I wasn't alone. I stared at the pregnancy test and watched as the double blue lines slowly appeared. My face began to get hot, my heart started beating faster. I was definitely pregnant. I couldn't even say it out loud without crying. I just walked out of the bathroom and held up the test. My roommates sat there shocked. "What are you going to do?" they asked. I wanted to curl up in a hole and forget the past hour. My introduction to motherhood was anything but glamorous.

The next day, the pregnancy was weighing in the back of my mind. I needed to tell my boyfriend. Would he think that I did this on purpose? I was pissed off, annoyed, and my mind was racing about all of the ways my life was going to change. I was in my fourth year at the University of South Dakota, an All-American swimmer, having the best season of my life. I had a carefree life, no responsibilities except going to class, performing at the meets, and partying with my friends. I was so used to doing whatever I wanted when I wanted. Life was a party! I had my whole life ahead of me, how could I have been so careless?

It was time to snap out of it and get back to performing mode. I was good at putting on a show for others. What were people going to think? How was I going to tell my parents, my boyfriend, my swim coaches? Would I be kicked off the swim team? I cared so damn much about what others thought of me. Not once did I stop to allow myself to process how I was feeling. My mind was racing in total chaos as I tried to find the answers. I was so afraid of being judged that I desperately searched for a way to sugarcoat the situation. I didn't like the uncomfortable feelings of shame and embarrassment, so as quickly as I felt them, I filled myself with distractions instead. If I kept myself busy enough, maybe, just maybe, the feelings would go away.

To make matters worse, I didn't even know if I liked kids. All of my friends were big-time athletes. I had only been around them the few times my three-year-old niece came to visit. I was the fun aunt who spoiled her and sent her back to her mom for the tough stuff. I was not prepared for diapers and PTA meetings. The thought of it all was completely overwhelming. I felt a knot in my stomach as I sat ashamed, embarrassed that I even was thinking this way. I should be happy, excited, and feeling all motherly and shit. Motherhood is supposed to be the best time of your life, right? Some mom I am going to make. "Snap out of it, Jenny! It's not about you anymore," I told myself. I had a baby to think about. I had to figure out how this would affect my relationship with my boyfriend, and how to finish school. It was time to stop being so selfish and put other people's needs before mine. That's what mom's do, right?

Surprisingly, my family took the news really well, but there were so many questions that I didn't have the answers to. My boyfriend asked "Do I want to keep the baby? Will we get married? Where will we live?" My dad also questioned whether or not I would drop out of school. All questions that needed answered. My mom sat quietly for probably the first time in her life. I remember thinking, "Why the fuck do I have to make all of the decisions, my boyfriend was just as much a part of this problem as I was? OMG, I just thought of my baby as a problem, that's not what I meant! Someone come take me out of my misery before I totally screw up this child." I needed to step up my game if I were going to succeed as a mom. One thing I knew for sure, I didn't want to get married just because I was pregnant. That was the last decision I made for myself for a very long time.

The plan was that we would stay in Vermillion so that I could finish my last two classes in my undergrad. I loved it there! The town reminded me of my hometown, small enough to make you feel like you were really a part of something. After weeks of looking at apartments and job hunting for my boyfriend, he threw a bombshell at me. He decided that we would be moving back to Wyoming, eight hours from Vermillion. I was paralyzed with anger. I tried to speak, but when I would open my mouth, the words just wouldn't come out. I tried to be strong, "Don't cry in front of him." I never wanted to be a coal miner's wife. Moving back to Wyoming felt so terribly wrong, but what choice did I have? I could stay in college with a brand-new baby and try to figure it out on my own? Or move back to my hometown and be with my family and boyfriend. For the first time in my life, I questioned whether or not I was actually capable of being an adult. I wish that I would have been stronger, to have the courage to stand up for myself and say "NO! I am staying, this is important to me." Instead, I sat like a coward packing my bags. I felt sick to my stomach as I logged onto my computer and dropped my college classes, knowing the likelihood of returning to finish my degree was slim to none. I had given up on my dream, I was such a failure.

The next few months were a whirlwind of changes. I felt completely out of control like someone else had taken the driver seat of my life. I found myself a college dropout, living in my parent's basement, with no direction or goals for myself at the age of twenty-two. My life as I knew it was completely unrecognizable and the baby hadn't even come yet. My happy-go-lucky persona was over as I sat in my parent's basement spiraling into a dark depression. The transformation was slow; it didn't happen all at once, but one small decision at a time. I had completely lost my identity.

I thought everything would change when my baby arrived. Watch any movie, or book on motherhood and you'll see… a golden shiny fairy waves a magic wand over the mom and everything is perfect. But it wasn't that easy for me. It was a gorgeous fall morning where I sat in my living room staring out the window, watching the leaves blow in the breeze. I finished the last drink of my lukewarm coffee, questioning my existence. My eyes were tired and dry from crying, up all night with a colicky baby. She was calm now; I held her as she slept. She looked absolutely perfect in my arms, but I still wasn't happy. This was a time where I should be feeling overfilled with joy, wanting to soak up every second. Instead, I stared out the window just wanting to be back in the world. I knew that I was going to be absolutely miserable for the rest of my life if I didn't do something. I hadn't felt this feeling in so long. The feeling was desire. This time instead of tuning it out as I had in the past, I leaned into it.

That afternoon, I ran into an old high school teammate. I found out she was coaching the swim team. Without hesitation, I offered to help out. I thought it would be a nice distraction. Although I was excited to be a part of something again, I didn't want to tell anyone, not yet. It was a huge time commitment and long weekends away from my baby girl. I wasn't ready to face the judgmental comments and eye rolls from other moms. It had been surprising the past few months how opinionated women could be. I was so annoyed and pissed off that I even felt like those other mom's needed or deserved an explanation as to why I was going to leave my baby and start working. It's my life, my family, my choice. So why did I feel so guilty? I was torn between fulfilling my duty to be that perfect Pinterest mom who bakes cookies every day and surrendering to my desire to get out of the house and work. Did it really make me a bad mom for wanting to leave my daughter and go back to work? Who even made that stupid rule?

The first day that I left my daughter with my mom, I thought I would be slapped with fear and mom guilt, but I wasn't. It felt like any other day. I didn't feel bad at all that I had left her. I felt safe and secure with my mom's support, and I knew she was in good hands. As I coached the kiddos from the pool deck, I was on such a high. I wasn't beating myself up for dropping out of college, or worried if my husband was going to be pissed when he got home because our house was a disaster. It just felt so natural.

Driving home, I started to feel the guilt creep in. Not because I left my baby to go back to work, but because I didn't feel bad about it. Other mom's that I had been comparing myself to, expressed so much sadness going back to work. They wanted so badly to be a stay at home mom, but they had to go back to work. Me, the exact opposite, my husband had a great job that would have allowed me to stay home, and he supported my decision no matter what. I slowly pulled around the corner into my parent's driveway, and as I put the car in park, I could see my dad holding my little girl through the window. He looked at her with such love and adoration, my heart melted. I instantly switched from second-guessing myself, to complete gratitude. This was a moment that would have been missed had I decided to stay home. I walked in the door, wrapped my arms around my dad and gave my daughter a kiss on the forehead. At that moment, I knew everything was going to be okay. Maybe I could have a fulfilling career and be a great mom after all?

I lost who I was when I became a mom. I changed who I was to fit this mold of who I thought I should be, and what I thought a good mom looked like. I gave my power away to those around me by not having the confidence to stand up for my desires. What I didn't realize was, that by disconnecting from my soul's purpose, I was modeling unrealistic expectations to all mothers around me, and to my very own babies who look up to me for guidance and support. My journey as a mom has included many cases where I allowed other's opinions to throw me off guard, knock me down, and leave me feeling like I'm a "bad mom." When I am truly in alignment with my soul's purpose, it's easier to recover from the falls.

A few months after my second daughter was born, I rented a cabin in the hills for the weekend with a few of my girlfriends. I was the only one who had kids and I was looking forward to enjoying a weekend away. The first night, all of us girls sat together in the hot tub, catching up, laughing and enjoying our time together. The conversation turned to families. One of my girlfriends had been struggling to get pregnant for a few years. She expressed how unfair life was, and how it was bullshit that she had done everything in the right order: dating, marriage, then kids; while other women who don't even want kids got pregnant right away without even trying. I sunk lower into my seat in the corner as if I could hide. My heart shattered into a million pieces. I felt attacked. I was one of the "other women." I prayed that the fog hovering over the hot tub and the dew on my face would disguise my tears. I allowed myself to get caught up in the moment and my shame and insecurities rushed back in. I didn't deserve to be a mom. I felt the need to explain myself, to prove that I was a good mom, and justify all the reasons that I was worthy. Instead, I shoved my feelings deep inside and pretended her words didn't hurt me. My daughters didn't need any explanation or justification, they just needed their perfectly imperfect mom to be there for them.

The words of a hurting woman can cut the deepest. They are the truest and most raw. These words can make even the strongest woman crumble to her knees. Everything she said was true, it really wasn't fair. I wanted her to be a mom as much as I loved being a mom. Every mother comes into this role in their own God-given unique way. I fell in love with an experience that I didn't even know I wanted, while some women wait their entire lives to become a mom. Just because my story isn't "normal" and looks different than others, it has no effect on the quality of our mothering abilities. Fuck being a "normal mom;" what does that even mean anyway? Motherhood really can be the best time of your life when you learn to quiet the voices and haters around you. There will always be someone around you who tries to make you feel less than, so you might as well enjoy yourself. It's time to let go of the victim mentality and old ideas of what motherhood should look like because the only person who can change your situation and lead you to a passionate purposeful life is yourself. Imagine raising empowered girls into women just by surrendering to your authenticity?

That would not be the last time I questioned my worthiness to be a mom or the decisions that I had made. This was only the beginning of my journey to becoming a supermom. Yeah, doubts and fears creep in and I start to feel overwhelmed, but then, I pause and surrender to my purpose. I tap into my mother's intuition where I just know what to do. Life is full of moments that test you and push you. It's in those moments where you grow stronger or spin into overwhelm.

My daughters are now eleven and nine. They both have such bold, rambunctious and awesome personalities that are completely different from one another. Together, we are entering a new phase of motherhood that is completely unfamiliar to us. They see that I am a different kind of mom and sometimes wonder why I can't just be like the other moms. When they see moms pulling off these elaborate magical-themed birthday parties and crafting all the sweet stuff; I am over here trying to get as many people to show up on short notice because I forgot to plan ahead. It's hard for them to not compare. I believe in having a ton of fun with my kids but also want to be a loving supportive role model. My view of what that looks like is different than other moms. I hate cooking and love my housekeeper; I haven't cleaned my own toilet in years! I may not be "Suzie Homemaker" but I will drive thousands of miles to watch their sports events. I will take an afternoon to play tourist and just do whatever they want to do, and sometimes we just curl up on the couch and watch a movie together.

One night after a long day at the office, I drove home debating whether I should stop at the store to buy groceries to make a quick dinner before rushing the girls to basketball practice, or order take out for the third night that week. Like any great mother, I opted for take-out. I slowly shuffled in the door, my hands overflowing with papers from work and to-go bags of fast food. I was immediately greeted by my now pre-teen daughter, who started spewing drama from her day in a teen language I hardly recognized, while my other daughter was ranting and raving, frantically trying to get her basketball gear in order, expressing how very displeased she was with my lack of creativity for dinner yet again. I pushed through the door and continued to the kitchen only to find a mess of homework and dirty dishes strung across the counter, all while my husband sat comfortably on the couch watching WWII documentaries. I felt myself creep back into my old patterns of chaos and overwhelm. I felt like screaming, and for a second, I was taken back to that moment in my college apartment when I questioned how I was going to make it as a mom if I was even capable. It took a minute to remember how far I had come. I remembered that it's okay to do things differently. I allowed myself to feel overwhelmed and stressed. Then I took a deep breath and smiled. I sat down with my oldest daughter to listen to her problems. Not to fix them, but to just be present with her while she worked through her chaos. My younger daughter bellied up to the island counter to scarf down her cheeseburger and fries. Instead of chaos, I felt gratitude. Thank God I get to be their mom.

We all do motherhood a bit differently and that's okay! There is no operator's manual to being a fantastic mom. Finding what works for you and learning to listen to your gut, your motherly intuition, the small voice of God guiding you; this will help free you from the judgment, and the overwhelm will begin to fade away. We need to stand together as women to break the mold of the old cookie-cutter ideas for how to be a great mom and start embracing our unique journeys! I have learned that old patterns and expectations of what it means to be a good mom resurface again with each stage of my girl's lives. I give myself grace and forgiveness for not being the mom I think I should be, while remembering as long as I stay true to my purpose, and tap into that, I will be exactly who my girls need me to be.

It takes courage to desire; to trust yourself enough to know what you want, and to take steps toward creating it. Listening to my soul calling gave me the strength to go start my own business, to finish my master's degree, and to travel the world. I have created a fulfilling career I love, where I have the time and money freedom to go on so many amazing adventures with my family. Whether you desire to create an online empire or be a stay at home mom, there is one thing I know for sure. Not only will you feel good as a mom by tapping into your authentic self, but you can have way more fun!

I am a strong-willed woman who would have been miserable had I continued to pretend I was something that I am not. I will never again pretend to be a perfect mom. I cuss, I cry, and I have a shit-ton of fun with my family! I love my perfectly chaotic life! Not everyone is as strong-willed as I am, to be able to push through when the world is telling you, "you can't." But we all have the potential to be!

Through the midst of the chaos and judgments of those around us, we can get into our heads so much that we can't hear the voice of God guiding and leading us. Listen to that soul calling inside you. Listen close, and chase that feeling like your life depends on it because it does!

*"Don't let the waves
of fear wash away
your authentic self."*

~ unknown

Tina Mast

Angel Communicator, Intuitive Medium, Theta Healer ®, Empath, Life and Wellness Coach, Mentor, and Author

Tina is much like you: wife, mother, sister, and friend. She has a strong desire to help and serve others. Her extremely positive outlook on life has helped her thrive and allowed her to encourage and help others along their journey. Her strong intuition has led her to trust her inner guide which has brought her new experiences and opportunities. Tina's mission is to be the person she herself needed when she was struggling to find her way. Ten years ago, she learned she was a medium, a divine gift which she uses to help people gain peace by delivering messages from those who have passed away.

Tina believes that we all need a safe place for healing to begin and when we support each other we can make that happen. She is eternally grateful to all the beautiful people and souls God has caused to cross her path, and for all the life experiences that have molded her into the woman she is today.

Tina has been heard on WDEL 101.7 Saturday Mornings Hot Spot with Frank Gregory. Workshops are being scheduled for 2020, as well as angel readings and life coaching sessions.

Email Tina at talkswithangels7@gmail.com.

Chapter Seven

Do It Afraid!

Tina Mast

Have you ever had a friend that has always brought you down? Can you relate to the one that is always negative and beating you up? Have you allowed that person to create doubt in yourself? A real Debbie Downer? That friend for me was fear. Fear was my Debbie Downer. It went everywhere with me and crushed my spirit every chance it could. Fear was that voice within me, a part of me. As I look back over my first 40 years, I let it rule my life. If you are like me, then you will relate to a journey that is fear-based and I hope to inspire you to, "do it afraid!"

Imagine being six years old and experiencing fear so intense you were frozen. I mean so immobilizing you had no idea what to do. There we were, my family, being led by a police officer into this cold, gray building, with cinder block walls crowding us in, dividing each of us sisters into separate rooms. I was all alone in the hallway, frightened beyond frightened, sitting on a wooden bench when Fear started to talk to me.

"This is all your fault! If you hadn't said anything, none of us would be here right now."

I told myself that when my uncles were touching me, they were just showing me how much they loved me. The voice of Fear continued, "Don't tell anyone that your dad does that to you too, or you'll never see your sisters again." Fear convinced me that no one cared that it didn't feel right. "Who cares about you and what you think?" I was just a kid and felt completely hopeless, like there wasn't anything I could do about any of it.

Fear made me start to doubt myself. Has that ever happened to you? You actually start thinking the things it's telling you are true. Things like, "Maybe it WAS my fault. I had let this happen." Or worse yet, "I caused all of this." I started to believe all the negative comments and eventually, I would even start the negative talk myself. I became very comfortable with the insults and constant uncertainty that fear instilled.

Time moved on and things didn't change much. I was still living with abuse, just in a different form as I got older. My best friend, fear, was still there, telling me I wasn't going to be able to do anything to change where I was or how I was being treated. I felt so defeated, constantly walking with my head down, not rocking the boat, afraid anything I did or said would get one of the adults angry and make them feel the need to teach me a lesson.

I laid face down with my tears staining the pillow, the skin on my bare bottom feeling the welts from the belt forming, feeling so powerless. A small, quivering voice in my head vowed to find a way to stop this. "As soon as I can get out of here, my life is going to change."

Fast forward several years. I was standing in front of a mirror, not feeling anywhere close to being beautiful in the dress I had always dreamed of. I was trying to convince myself that I'd make a beautiful bride, that I would soon be living the life I always thought about when I was eighteen. What I was really thinking was, "I'm moving out and fear isn't coming with me this time."

I figured with this new relationship I was finally going to make something of myself. As we started painting and fixing up the house, changes were happening inside of me and I was feeling happy. I felt like things were finally going my way! I wasn't afraid anymore and truly felt positive that I could make life good, even amazing! Yes, I had the power to create a world that was the exact opposite of what I had lived in before.

All too soon, I figured out how out of touch I was. Guess who came back? That's right. Fear. Debbie Downer had managed to sneak in when I wasn't looking. This time the conversation was, "What's your problem? Why are you acting so weird? Shut up! Just do what you're told. You're a wife and a mother now, there's nothing more for you." An overwhelming sense of sadness and doom rushed over me and my heart once again.

With an exhausted breath and a heavy heart, my spirit had finally given up and accepted the truth; I'll never be able to get away. How did I let this happen? How had I failed to see the signs? When did I allow people to treat me so badly? I felt like I was watching a movie or witnessing someone else's life. You know, when you can see it clearly and say to someone, "That's not good for you, that person isn't going to make you happy."

God knew I was unhappy, hurting, depressed and feeling broken. People would say things like, "Everything happens for a reason," or, "It's all a part of God's plan." Well, God's plan sucks! How could He do this to me? Why would God keep putting me in these situations? Why would He make me live a life where I'm always afraid and depressed? That doesn't sound like a loving God to me. Why isn't He helping me get out of this? I had to find the answers!

As I'm asking all these questions, fear was following me around, taking notes. Then something odd happened. Fear's role had changed.

What was once the weight that continually held me down, now became my motivator. It was like a switch flipped. Things started to stir inside of me and new thoughts were coming to me in a way that was totally unfamiliar. The dialogue went from, "You can't leave, you can't take your kids from the only home they've ever known," to, "Aren't you afraid that if you don't do something now, you'll be stuck in this forever? Aren't you afraid that no one will stand up for you? If you don't start to love yourself enough, no love or light will ever be able to come in."

While my questions were being answered by a higher power, suddenly my annoyingly negative, constant companion changed perspective and gave me hope.

Now it was convincing me to take ownership of my life and it propelled me to take some action. "Get out of this life you created, there is nothing to be afraid of. You can have the life you always dreamed of if you really want it."

Once the action was in place, God was on a roll. I was seeing things about myself I now knew. There was an alignment of people coming into my life, amazing people who actually encouraged me.

My broken heart was mending and I felt guided to a relationship with this exceptional man. He was warm and kind, generous and hard-working. I wanted to give my heart to this man, but I didn't want to lose myself in the process. I had to trust and have a deeper faith in myself. I wanted to know myself better, however, I had to find out who I was. The little glimpses I would get of her were not enough for me to be confident to give myself to another person yet and I felt it wouldn't be fair either. I set out to find out who I am.

I began asking myself silly questions like, "What kind of cereal do I like? What's my favorite color? What's my favorite food?" Questions that slowly evolved into, "What do I want to do with my life? What will make me truly happy?" Questions like these allowed me to find out who I truly was, deep down.

I loved what I found.

I found someone who loved being around people, loved laughing, who loved fuzzy socks and a hot cup of coffee. I was so inspired by this woman, I wanted to let her out, let her shine! Then Debbie showed up. She was terrified and afraid that I wouldn't want her anymore. "Would anyone like us now?" I took a deep breath, found some inner strength and you know what, I did it! I did it afraid! That's right, I did it afraid! Fear was no longer going to stop me, even if it was with me. I would hear Debbie talk in my head and I said, "Let's be friends and move in with me. Let's create a beautiful life together."

One of the things I learned about myself was that I wanted to travel and soon I was on a trip with my sister. She always wanted to go to Sedona so the new adventurous me said, "Let's go!" On our first day, we stumbled upon this park and decided to check it out. As we were walking along the riverbank, I had this overwhelming feeling I was being watched. Maybe you know what I'm talking about? The feeling where you're sure there's someone behind you, only to turn around and no ones there. But you know they were, you could feel it! The whole thing made me feel uncomfortable and a little freaked out. I wasn't enjoying the walk, so I told my sister I wanted to leave. "There goes Debbie again, ruining the fun," I thought. Or was it just something unfamiliar to me that made me feel so scared?

The next day, we had arranged a hike around the red rocks with a guide. A few minutes into the walk, my sister's back was bothering her so we decided to sit for a minute. I sat down and couldn't stop looking at this stunning nature around us. The majestic red rocks were jutting out here and there. There were spots with trees; other spots that were completely bare. The sun was shining on the one mountain, like rays from heaven and it just took my breath away seeing the colors across the mountainside light up like a vibrant painting, just for me. I lifted my head and took a deep breath to smell the flowers and trees. Everything had an aliveness in the air I had never experienced before. I rubbed some red dirt on my fingers so I could ground myself. I couldn't believe that I was in a place as magnificent as this! Pinch me! I let myself get completely immersed in this magical vortex. It felt so grounding that it made me feel like I had come home. I knew I wasn't alone.

I allowed myself to be vulnerable to all my senses. I didn't fight them or question them. Everything seemed to envelop me into a serenity that I never knew existed. Emotions welled up inside of me. I had to take a minute to thank God for this beautiful place, for guiding me to this moment full of peace and for lifting me out of the hell I had endured.

As I was quietly savoring the moment, I felt that strong feeling that someone was watching us again. The same intense feeling I'd had in the park the day before. The presence was strong.

I turned around to see who it was and just like before, no one was there. I mentioned it to the tour guide and he said, "Ask them their name."

I was like, what? "Ask who?"

"The person you keep turning around to see. Ask them their name." The tour guide waited for me to do what he had suggested. I felt completely silly but I did it anyway. When I asked, a very specific name came to me. I turned to my sister with wide eyes and said, "His name is Pudintain."

This word probably means nothing to you, but to me and my sister, it could only be one person. Pop-Pop. He used to say this silly poem. "What's my name? Pudintain. Ask me again and I'll tell you the same." We both started to cry. When I turned away from her to look back at the mountain, the most amazing thing ever happened. I saw all these angels, everywhere! I saw people in the trees, animals all over and colors I had never seen before! It was like the part in Wizard of Oz when Dorothy goes from seeing black and white to seeing in full color. I couldn't believe what I was seeing. How did I miss this? How did I not see all of this before? Debbie Downer was nowhere to be found. She transformed into Dorothy and the magic was going to take me home, the place I always longed for. That place within me that was a deep sense of peace.

With a shaky voice, I began to describe what I saw, all the while not believing what I was seeing. I paused, searching to find the words to give these visions justice. As I turned to look at our guide, I saw this dark-skinned, young Indian chief dressed all in white. My sister said she couldn't see him but felt a strong energy where I described him to be. None of this made any sense to me. "How can she not see him? He's right there in plain sight!" I thought to myself.

Then this calm and grounding presence filled me. A peace that easily pushed fear to the side and filled my soul. Such a beautiful, almost tingling sensation from head to toe. As we left that magnificent mountainside, I prayed that I would never lose that feeling. Unknowingly at that time, God answered my prayer. Not the one I just prayed. The one I had prayed as a child cowering in the corner, as the wife who was just a shell of a woman, as a mother who felt she was failing her children. "Lord help me to leave this life of fear and become the woman you truly made me to be, inside and out." I felt such a feeling of inner peace, a knowing and understanding that these visions were part of my purpose on this planet. I saw a glimpse of who I could become. I was enthralled in a magical awe that lifted me so high I opened my arms and heart to receive this blessing. That feeling still continues to bless me to this day.

I had grown so tired of fighting who I was because people didn't understand me or I made them uncomfortable. Honestly at times, this gift has made ME uncomfortable. But the true magic in life happens outside of our comfort zone. The so-called comfort zone I'd been living in had never felt all that comfortable to me anyways. I made a decision then and there that I was done with shutting myself off, finished with trying to be something to everyone. No longer would I try to be someone I wasn't in order to make someone else happy.

The days and weeks that followed that trip were exciting and scary all at the same time. I was seeing and hearing things I had never experienced before. Random people were coming up to me and would just start talking. They didn't even say hello or introduce themselves, they were just talking and talking fast. So fast I had to tell them to slow down so I could understand them. Turns out, they weren't people as you would know them, they were angels. Boy, was I surprised! They were people who had passed away, people who now knew I could see and hear them. They excitedly told me all these stories and messages they so desperately wanted their loved ones to hear. How was I going to process all of this? It was quite overwhelming at first.

Have you ever seen the movie *"Ghost"*? Think about the part when Patrick Swayze finds Whoopi Goldberg and talks to her to see if she can hear him. Remember her reaction when she actually heard him? Her eyes got really big and she freaked out! He was jumping around asking her if she could hear him. When he realized she could, he desperately started telling her how she had to find his wife because he had something to tell her. He was frantic to have her deliver this message. I laugh a little when I think of her response. She was like 'Oh hell no! Get out of my head! Stop bothering me!' Remember that part? Well, that was a little like how it was for me.

At first, I felt bombarded with these new visitors. Through mentors and training, I learned how to talk to them and ask them to slow down. With training, I was able to ask them to wait until I was with their loved ones before giving me their messages. Some of the messages were simply, "Tell her I love her; I miss him or please make sure they know I'm okay." Some knew that the person receiving the message wouldn't believe what they were hearing so they would say something specific or give me a name. Wow, this was crazy! How was I going to deliver these messages?

There was this one time when I was sitting with two women. I felt this strong feeling from someone on the other side wanting to let them know he was there. It took me a couple of minutes to build up the courage to say something. I asked them if they knew anyone named Dustin. He had given me his name so they would know it was him. They didn't say anything to me, just looked at each other with wide eyes. I'm being patient, thinking they're going to say something, just give them a minute. Nothing. Dustin starts pleading with me to say more. I finally said, "He wants you to know he's okay. He loves you and he's sorry for not being smarter with his life." The younger woman put her face in her hands and started to cry. Her friend said her boyfriend had passed away from a drug overdose six weeks ago today. On our way there she was saying how she just wanted to know if he was okay. I understood at that moment that this was part of who I was, the messenger God designed me to be. A blessing for many who would need this peace.

I believe this was part of His plan all along. I realized that in searching and getting to know the part of myself I was so curious about, God revealed to me the woman He truly created me to be. Had I denied who I was and not said something to those women that day, I wouldn't have been true to myself or to the gifts I have so graciously been given. It was time to stop allowing what other people thought control me and become who I was destined to be. I'm proud of who I am. I'm excited about my life! I'm curious to see the woman I'll be five years, ten years, even twenty years from now.

Rising above all that was dealt to me took all the strength I had and some I didn't. I knew that if I continued to live my life in fear, I would never live out the life I was meant to have. I promised myself that fear wouldn't ever control me again. Does it creep back in every once in a while? You bet. But it doesn't live inside my home or my head any longer. I did it afraid. There may be times where I need to fearfully do it again. If I do, now I have the confidence and peace knowing I can always be me, no matter what. So do it afraid! I did!

"*Courage is fear*

who has said

her prayers"

~ Dorothy Bernard

Jacqueline Wands

Jacqueline was born and raised in Long Island, NY. She now lives in Florida with her husband and their golden retriever, Colb. She has worked for non-profit organizations her entire professional life, and retired from working for the American Cancer Society as Director of Patient Services in Suffolk County, NY. She has been a seeker of enlightenment since she first climbed trees in the woods as a child and continues to follow that path today.

Jacqueline continues to challenge herself by seeking new experiences, traveling, and believes that paying our blessings forward goes a long way toward creating a better world for ourselves and others. Jacqueline and her husband volunteer with Unity Church and Family Promise.

Email Jacqueline at Jacqueline.Wands@gmail.com

Chapter Eight

The Girl Who Climbed Trees

Jacqueline Wands

I was stunned, crying when suddenly time stopped. It was a day when I just didn't understand my feelings of anger and a cascade of emotion enveloped me, seemingly out of nowhere. I didn't understand.

I was a new mom. My 18-month-old child was inquisitive, curious and creative on most days. On this day, he was fretting, crying and not in a good mood. I remember his big blue eyes gazing at me as he was sitting on the steps to the second floor of our home. Out of nowhere, and much to my surprise, he threw his baby shoe directly at me! It hit me in the face and I immediately reacted. Without thinking, I threw it back at him. His little face immediately had a look of shock, and he began crying harder. OMG! What did I just do? I couldn't stop myself. I stood there frozen, stunned, and time stopped. I was horrified and I looked back at him, tears in my eyes, feeling helpless. Instantly I ran to him, picked him up and began rocking him back and forth.

I thought to myself, "Mothers don't respond like this to their children, do they?" NO! I silently screamed at myself. Good mothers don't do this! In that very moment, full of shame and guilt, I knew that something was not okay. How could I do this to my baby? It was not a normal reaction.

Why did I feel this way? I had a wonderful husband, a house in the suburbs and a beautiful baby boy. I felt completely devastated. However, something also shifted in me. I somehow knew something wasn't 'right' but didn't know what it was as the words, "You're a bad mother," kept playing over and over in my head. It felt like something cracked inside. I was trying to create a perfect life, be a perfect mom, a perfect wife, perfect everything and I realized in that moment it wasn't working.

I had no idea then my life would follow a path of seeking to find "myself". Searching for the feelings that I experienced as a little girl climbing up to the top of those tree branches. Feelings of freedom! I felt connected and joyful in those moments. Years would go by searching for those feelings, searching for a way back or, perhaps, a way to get away from the stories I had told myself. Growing up, I always felt I needed to be perfect, to be the good girl. I believed I needed to care more about other peoples' feelings than my own. For some reason, I believed I needed to make up for other people's deficiencies, especially my parents. So how did I get to this moment with my own son, feeling so far away from being a perfect mom?

I believe there are moments that define our lives, where we go from one place to another in a matter of seconds. Moments when we step out of the life we are living and into a new life that is totally different. Our lives are never the same after these events, and we can never go back, as much as we might desire to.

Maybe it was divine order, but shortly after I threw the shoe back at my son, I saw an ad from the local university's Psychology Department. They were asking for moms with children to participate in some sessions to help the students gain skills working with families. Little did I know one day I would be part of an organization called Family Promise at Unity Church.

I felt like I was looking for "something", but I had no idea what. While I wasn't even sure what this group was exactly, I signed up for it. With more than a little anxiety, I walked into the room where the group was meeting. The facilitator had a friendly open attitude and talked about feelings, our anger and how we could live less stressful lives. I looked around the room, a typical cold classroom with all the rows of seats, and thought to myself, "Are they all getting it?" I had no idea, not a clue, what she was talking about! Did they?

Surely none of this was about me? It was interesting in some ways, but I couldn't relate to it. I didn't have a clue why we had to do exercises like counting to 10 before we reacted to stressful situations. Every time I walked into those classes,

I felt confused, especially with the discussions around feelings. Definitely the discussions on anger! Anger scared me. I avoided expressing anger at all costs in my life. I was the people pleaser, the perfect little girl. We were encouraged to think about how anger had been expressed in each of our homes when we were children. I remembered there were infrequent but explosive bouts of anger expressed by my father. Those moments had scared me as a child, and I learned to avoid anger at all costs.

I used to question if this group would help me realize things about myself I didn't know. The answer? Absolutely! I was about to learn about codependency and how I had lost myself. I remembered not knowing how and being unable to ask for help when I needed it. I was perplexed and confused about that process. Over the next year of classes, I did my best to understand how to connect my feelings with my thoughts. I began reading self-help books. I already had a collection of books about death and dying. My mother-in-law had recently been diagnosed with lung cancer. I had gotten the books because I wanted to know how to explain this to a two-year-old, if that was even possible?

The next year, everything drastically changed for me. I was thrown into a shocking place of existence, filled with grief and loss for myself and my family. Things would change in a way I never suspected and never would have chosen.

It was a beautiful morning in February, the sun was shining across clear, cold blue skies. If you know me, I love my coffee, and it was brewing in the air today. I met a friend at a local coffee shop that morning, before an appointment at my hair salon. I recall chatting with her about my Dad and sharing how worried I was about how he had been acting the week before. He hadn't seemed himself.

My friend and I went our separate ways. Right after I arrived in the salon parking lot, my husband pulled up in our car. Watching him come towards me my body immediately tensed up. I could see by the look on his face something was wrong. Fear washed over me. His mouth opened and words started coming out. Time stopped when he said, "Your father has died. They found him behind the house, in the woods." I started to scream when I heard him say, "He hung himself in a tree." What? I saw myself falling, a big black hole swallowing me alive. A rush of feelings ran through me - fear, grief and explosive anger that I could not control. I felt like my head was going to explode. The pain I was experiencing was blinding, the shock beyond believable. In a tree? Dad was gone? How does counting to ten help now, someone please tell me?

I experienced something at that moment that immediately changed my life. It would define me for years and ultimately save me, although I didn't know it at the time. This traumatic event shook me to the core and caused me to question everything I believed about myself and how life was supposed to work. I questioned, "If he loved me, how could this happen? How could someone do this to *me*?" I had so many mixed feelings, from shock, confusion, and shame, to anger and rage.

How will I survive? I had no coping mechanisms for my father of 57 leaving me. I couldn't make sense of any of it. He was so young.

For a long time after my dad died, I would wish that I could go back and reverse time. In the mornings, before I first opened my eyes, in that twilight space before I was fully awake, I would believe that it hadn't happened, that he hadn't killed himself. Then reality would hit me, and the despair and grief would rush in, suffocating me.

None of what happened made sense. I always remember my dad being so strong. When he was young, he took a chance and emigrated from the Netherlands to the United States by himself. He was young, incredibly brave, smart and creative. He always had this amazing energy, which seemed bottomless.

As time went by after his death, we came to realize he had been suffering from clinical depression. He had lost interest in the hobbies that normally made him happy, but he would never tell us why. His appetite changed and over time he wouldn't eat the foods he used to love. He had become irritable and anxious, even with things that had never bothered him before. Even though he had been exhibiting many of the classic symptoms, at the time none of us were aware of what they really meant. Like many families I know, we had "family rules." You did not talk about or tell anyone your 'personal business.' You didn't share your pain or sadness. We were taught to keep it to ourselves, to not ask for help from anyone else.

How could such terrible things happen if I was following all the "rules"? How do these things happen to good people? The questions flowed through my head. Endlessly I questioned my life and my perfectionism. I wondered if I would survive all these shattered feelings.

Now, what was I supposed to do? I had no idea what I really wanted in life even though I had a beautiful child and a wonderful husband. I should be satisfied, right? I was going through the motions and could not understand why I wasn't happy. I knew my husband loved me and we had a beautiful family and home. Isn't this what they teach little girls? That this is what it's all about? Get married, have a beautiful home, make a beautiful family, and live happily ever after.

Over the next year, I felt like I had fallen into a big black hole. Every insecurity, every fear, and inadequacy showed up. How would I prevent my son from being affected by this in his life? Was that even possible when the world turns upside down?

As I reflected on my life, I could not stop the feelings of horrendous guilt. I felt like I should have been able to prevent what happened to my father. I should also be grateful for all I had, right?

I didn't understand all of the feelings I was having and judged myself harshly. I wasn't able to accept how I was feeling because, at that time, I couldn't even accept myself. But feelings just are, aren't they? We carry them with us, the unfinished business of our families and those who have come before us. I was carrying all of this baggage for years, stuffing it down inside of me because the message had been that you don't talk about any of this "stuff." That was what I had learned. I also began to see how, for generations, the women in my family had used food to mask their feelings. I wanted to understand why and try to make sense of it all.

There were times I felt comatose, like I was just going through the motions. For so long I had believed that by doing well in school, and being the "perfect daughter" meant I had self-worth. However, I didn't realize how conditional all those expectations really were. That was why I never really felt good about myself or felt truly happy. I was basing my self-worth on other peoples' views of how I was supposed to behave. As a child, I was sensitive, creative and talented, but something else was missing from my life. I just didn't know that it was "ME!"

My mother was also very smart and creative and didn't have an opportunity to fulfill her own potential. She was taking care of three little children in a very stressful and tough time while my father worked all the time. She didn't drive and didn't work outside the home. I can't even imagine what she was feeling inside. They both taught me the value of hard work, just not how to create balance. I, too, would learn how to zealously overwork, over achieve, just about killing myself to be the best employee in every job. I had no idea how disconnected I was from myself or my body. I just wanted to live up to what others expected of me, even though at the same time I was rejecting myself. The mirror was not my friend. Even though I had won the contest in high school for "Most Likely to Be Miss America," I only saw flaws when I looked at myself. It just got worse in college. I was stressed and filled with self-loathing. I was completely frightened and didn't know how I would manage going away by myself or taking care of myself. How would I do this? When the girls upstairs in my dorm introduced me to a way to eat everything I wanted to and not "get fat", I thought this was the best thing going! Little did I know (because there was no name for it back then) that I was about to embark upon a journey of using "bulimia," as a way of coping with stress and my unresolved feelings about my body. It tempered all the feelings I had that I couldn't name or understand, even though I wasn't aware of any of the repercussions.

Eventually I learned how addictions go hand in hand with dysfunctional families and are handed down for generations. I would also reach out and connect with a Survivors of Suicide group, mustering up the courage to walk into the meeting, really out of desperation. Listening to the levels of honesty of the people sharing took my breath away. It was in those moments that I realized I could relate to the stories. At the same time, I struggled with finding the right words to describe how I felt. When I decided to start individual therapy, I knew it would be a huge step in my life. I believed I was doing this for my son but eventually came to realize that it was the first step on a road that saved my life.

I was shocked to hear my therapist share with me in the first session that she believed I was exhibiting suicidal ideation, meaning that I was talking like a person at risk for suicide. I was so disconnected from myself that I didn't even understand what she meant at first. Therapy was slow going, one step forward, two steps back. I had never had the experience of talking truthfully about myself and my feelings or being with someone who gave unconditional acceptance of what I shared. It was incredibly important for the healing process to find people I could trust, groups I could feel comfortable in so that I could get the support I needed. I also think what kept me going was my seeking nature, along with my curiosity to see where my journey would lead me.

If you are reading this story, maybe you can relate to some or all of it. If so, then it was written to help you on your journey. Know this, I had to learn how to re-parent myself and it took time. I have gone to twelve-step programs, read tons of self-help books and focused on how I could be a better parent for my son. We all need to find our why, our reason for being able to change our circumstances, change our stories and our lives. Part of that, I have come to believe, is because we inherently have a burning desire to search for our authentic self despite our circumstances or the way we may have grown up.

I was driven to continue to move forward even though I often felt like giving up. I have often asked myself where that tenacity and inner desire to survive came from. While I am not totally sure, I think there is an inner desire within some people to persist despite everything. For me, there was a spiritual component, a connection I felt with something greater than myself. I felt it that first time I climbed those trees in my back yard. Going higher and higher, trying to get closer to something I could only feel with my heart. I also knew that I wanted to be an example for my son in how to live a life connected to both our mind and body and to be able to create our story on our own terms.

One of the most powerful lessons of the journey was coming to understand that I wasn't alone. To understand that there were other people who could relate to what I had experienced in my life. We can all feel alone and isolated when we don't feel that we are understood. We can believe there is shame in our stories, and that people won't like us if we share our flaws and our fears. It can be as simple as telling the truth about how we feel, but even that can seem daunting if we don't believe we are good enough.

I learned that it is in the sharing of the stories that we find hope. It is in the sharing of our stories that we can see that we are more alike than different. Those stories are a bridge to our past, to those who have come before us, and we are connected by those threads on our journeys. As women, many of us have learned to focus outside of ourselves, on caring and helping others, on thinking more about others than ourselves.

And while those qualities have a positive value, if we hold onto them at the expense of ourselves, we do ourselves a disservice. And we role model this behavior for our children who will carry it on into their own lives.

I have learned that I am worth it, that my voice and my opinion matter, that I have choices, even if I don't always like them at any given moment. I have learned that my spiritual life is important, that there is something greater than myself and that I have had angels support and guide me my entire life, always present, never giving up on me. Those angels come in human form on this earth too, in each and every person who shares their truth for the benefit of others. I have learned that our thoughts can become our reality and have incredible power in the choices we make in our lives. If we believe we can't do it, we won't! I learned that it IS possible to change, and that change is a process of putting one foot in front of the other, one step at a time. I look back now on my life and know that I was supported by a power greater than myself on my journey. I have also been fortunate to come to believe that we need to do the things that we fear. I have been able to walk back onto a stage after a 50-year absence, done some comedy on stage, climbed over the Andes at 17,000 ft. I believe that it's important to pay it forward and I do that by volunteering for many different organizations. I use the skills I learned in my life to help others. Working with families and children that are homeless also gives me a chance to offer unconditional support and practice self-acceptance in ways that I didn't give myself. This is coming full circle back to myself.

I might not have made it to the place I am today if it wasn't for the love of so many people. The love of my son, my husband

and all those who have supported me including my mentors. Add in God's grace and a fierce inner courage that said "I want to live!"

I love the quote: "Courage is fear who has said her prayers." It takes enormous courage to change. And even more to recognize the need for change in ourselves and to take that first step. I can acknowledge that for myself today. Those that shared their own stories of truth gave me courage. They continue to do so. And like that little girl who courageously climbed those tall trees when she was little to find those feelings of connection, joy, and wonder, we can own and claim all that and more in our lives every day. I wish for all that, and more for each one of you. The journey continues.

"Some women choose to follow men, and some choose to follow their dreams. If you're wondering which way to go, remember that your career will never wake up and tell you that it doesn't love you anymore."

~ Lady Gaga

Marianne St Clair

As an internationally acclaimed muse, Marianne St. Clair is an expert at leading people through the Expanded Embodiment - Multi-Sensory Experiences. Moving them out of their heads and into their sensual bodies so that they reclaim their 5 Essential P's - Peace, Pleasure, Power, Purpose and Prosperity.

Marianne is a woman who not only learns the skills necessary for this work but she is one of the few who are truly dedicated to doing the inner work herself so that she shows up with a deeply spiritual presence that immediately puts people at ease.

Marianne is an internationally recognized Feminine Empowerment Coach, Published Author, International Speaker, and Leader. She amplifies women's process of reclaiming their Sovereignty in all capacities - sexually, emotionally, financially, creatively, and relationally and has taught these techniques to thousands of people around the world.

www.mariannestclair.com
Fb.me/mariannestclair
LinkedIn.com/mariannestclair

Chapter Nine

Reclaiming my Sovereignty

Marianne St Clair

I gently slid the skinny strap off my shoulder and untucked my arm from my nightgown, allowing it to cascade slowly down my skin, leaving my entire body bare and exposed to the coolness of the night's air.

I turned around to catch a faint glimpse of my nude body in the mirror as I stopped there for a brief moment to catch my breath. My body was changing ever so quickly, from my breasts enlarging, to my face becoming fuller. I was packing on some new weight which increased my curves. I had just turned 40 years old and certainly not the spring chicken I once was. Things were now sagging and just not as perky as they used to be.

As I stand here now, I recall a time when I was a seven-year-old little girl making sand castles on the beach and frolicking along the water line picking up seashells. I didn't have a care in the world and felt the innocence that most little girls that age should feel. Unbeknownst to me, this would be the night that changed my life forever.

It was a hot and humid summer evening when my mother, her boyfriend and I were camping on the sandy beach. I spent all day picking up seashells, tossing them into my bucket. I built the most beautiful sand castle, lined with my shells and pretended that I was a magical fairy princess who lived there.

As time went on, my mom's boyfriend had carved out a hole in the sand and built us a campfire. I sat on a chair and put my stick into the fire to cook my hotdog. Oh boy, I couldn't wait! It would soon be time to roast marshmallows and I absolutely loved watching as the fire turned my marshmallow brown. I giggled with the excitement and anticipation of making and eating s'mores. I twirled and danced around the fire, singing songs. The wind whisked through my hair as I bounced all around, dancing. I loved feeling so special and how all the attention was on me. My mom and her boyfriend kept saying how cute I was, as I was having a blast in my own world.

As the sun began to set, like most tropical hot Florida evenings, the bugs began to appear. Those no-see-um bugs began to bite my legs and arms, and no matter how much I swatted, they continued to annoy me. "No-see-um's" are these little, tiny, gnat-like bugs that are pesky beyond your wildest imagination, turning what was a beautiful evening into one of my life's greatest nightmares.

It wasn't long until we all scurried to finish up what we were doing outside, making a mad dash to take refuge inside the camper that was on the back of my mom's boyfriend's truck

A whole day of playing in the sun and saltwater had taken its toll on me. I was tired and exhausted. Yawning, sleepy, and barely able to keep my eyes open, I couldn't wait to crawl into bed.

The warm sunlight was slipping away into the darkness of night. The air was still. It was extremely stuffy in the camper, so before getting into bed, my mom dressed me in a simple T-shirt and a pair of panties.

The camper was quite small. It had only one bed which was the dining room table that converts into a full-size bed. All three of us would be sleeping there. My mom crawled in first next to the wall where there was a window, next was her boyfriend in the middle, and lastly, me on the outside edge of the bed. We all three snuggled and said our good nights.

I drifted off into dreamland and was fast asleep until…

I felt an urge to pee. I didn't wake up fully at first. I was groggy and still half asleep, in a somewhat twilight state. As the urge continued to grow stronger, I awoke more. I felt some sort of pressure. I felt something moving down between my legs. What was happening? This felt strange and weird. I had never felt anything like this. I was now fully awake and could feel my mom's boyfriends' whiskers pressing against my back near my shoulders. I smelled his breath as he breathed hot air on my neck. He was playing with my personal sacred private space.

Oh no! I was scared. I froze and couldn't move.

A rush of thoughts kept racing around in my head and I just couldn't get them to stop. I wanted them to stop. I wanted to go back to sleep and pretend this never happened. Was I dreaming? Was this really happening?

Why was he touching me? Why was this older man touching me down there?

I had been told by my mom and grandmother to never let anyone touch or play with my privates and I was. So why was this happening to me?

He told me to be quiet and he would make me feel really good. It did feel good. It felt really good. I liked it. He was making me feel good in a way I couldn't comprehend.

I felt really confused. My brain felt as if it stopped working and shut down. I froze. I couldn't move, speak, or think.

I knew this was really bad and wrong but I liked it. I felt dirty.

I felt like those no-see-ums bugs were right there in the bed with me, and they were biting me, yet no one else could see them. My mom was on the other side of him, fast asleep. She didn't see what was happening. Why aren't you awake, mom? Why aren't you stopping him and protecting me?

He continued for what seemed like a long time and then he stopped. With both of his hands, he pulled my panties back up from where he had slid them down. He then proceeded to turn back over and began hugging my mom. That felt really strange to me. Deep down, I felt empty and confused. I felt drained. Finally, I fell back asleep.

The next morning, nobody said anything. Not him. Not me. It was like the no-see-em bugs were symbolic, as I look back. They were there biting, and yet no one noticed that all this happened. No one saw it or addressed it, but they hurt. I didn't tell my mom because I didn't want to upset her. I didn't know how she would react. I was too terrified to tell her because what if she didn't believe me? So I kept it all bottled up to myself.

My life changed forever in that hour. He took something from me that I would never get back. He took my innocence. I had not only lost my virginity, it was stolen from me.

This event was swept under the rug, the lack of understanding and explanation of this trauma began an unfortunate cycle of seeking attention for love. In turn, marinating a cluster fuck of unhealthy habits which would resurface time and time again throughout my love life.

Later on in life, I began to feel the all-too-familiar sexual confusion that I did that night when I was seven-years-old.

Once again, the nasty monster named 'trauma' decided to roar its voice. I began to look for attention. I searched for the affection and love of a former sweetheart, but the key to his heart was nowhere to be found.

One quiet night, while lying in bed, I inched closer to him. I could tell he was facing away, that his back was turned towards me. I felt so warm and fuzzy in that split second until...

Out of nowhere, he took my arm and flung it off of him. He shouted, "Quit it! Cut that shit out!"

I was stunned. I felt traumatized all over again. My body became stiff and I could barely breathe. I froze in a state of shock.

As the sudden turn of events unfolded before my eyes, a variety of thoughts flooded my mind. "What did I do to make him not want me or desire me?" I had never had anyone reject me like this. It felt like those bugs were after me again, that symbol that followed me in life. I felt like I had done something wrong and it was all my fault. I asked him what was wrong, and he just muttered something under his breath and dismissed me as if I was a dog.

I felt so alone and ashamed.

I moved over to my side of the bed. I was heartbroken and confused. I could feel the water starting to well up in my eyes and then slowly drip down my cheek. Then another and another tear cascaded down until a waterfall of tears were beginning to form a wet spot on the sheets. I tried to be quiet and not make too much noise, but I couldn't help the sniffles that followed as I began to curl up into a fetal position.

I lay there awake for the entire night replaying the scene over and over in my head, and every time I did the flood gates opened again. I wanted to wake him up and talk to him about why he did what he did. But I didn't.

Once again, I didn't say anything. I suffered all night in agony until he finally woke up the next morning. I didn't bother him. I only felt the intense pain of rejection. My heart and my body shut down. I was crushed.

I got up early and I was in the living room when he walked out. I looked like hell. My eyes were swollen from a night of crying. I greeted him with a smile, and I asked him if we could discuss what happened last night. In a dismissive voice, he uttered adamantly, "No!" He didn't want to talk about it nor was it open for discussion.

I was not given the opportunity to understand or discuss what happened. It was as if he turned to stone. He turned away, stopped making eye contact with me, and sat there like I didn't even exist. I felt ignored, misunderstood, invalidated, and just plain hurt.

What was I going to do? I was heartbroken!

I started shutting down and separating myself from my soul. I didn't fight back or make him stop. I just gave my power away.

I spiraled into a never-ending void of depression and misery.

I seemed to be looking at the shell of what once was a vivacious woman, beaming with vitality. Where was Marianne? Who was this ghostly woman that I was looking at now in the mirror, at 45 years of age?

Over time, I had become desensitized and nearly numb to my body and my life. I became very guarded towards stronger people because I felt inferior. It was easier to block my emotions and feelings out than to process every ounce of pain and hurt I felt. I had kept these unexpressed and internalized emotions bottled up until they eventually began to physically eat away at me. Such as those damn bugs, the no-see-ums. REMOVE - repetitive

I went to extremes to guard myself against feeling more pain. I had unconsciously stunted my own physical feelings because of the violations both sexually and emotionally. I stopped paying attention to my bodily sensations, which are connected to my emotions. Things like that lump in my throat when I felt sadness, the burning in my chest when I was angry, or the faint fluttering in my stomach that meant I was anxious. Tuning in to my body had always been my guide and helped me figure out what I needed. It prevented me from doing or saying something I might later regret. It was easier not to feel the pain of not being wanted or desired than to continue feeling the pain from being rejected.

The more numb I became, the more shut down and turned off I felt in my own body.

The more dead I felt inside, the more I felt I needed to have sex with someone to uplift me and make me feel better. I was in a relationship that wasn't giving me those dopamine highs I needed. I wasn't feeling satisfied as a woman with a huge, soft heart. I began to find other ways. I used food, television, work, the internet, my kids, and many other methods, as ways to get my fix and feed what was missing. Most addictions can be traced back to some sort of early trauma, be it sexual or another form of trauma; drugs, sex, gambling, food, alcohol, and even workaholism. I could now make sense why it seemed so much easier to use something to numb out like these common methods people were substituting for their high fix.

I stayed in the relationship and had not realized how dead I had become. I compromised my health and happiness by neglecting to take a closer look at my life. I wasn't taking responsibility for my life, yet.

I buried myself into taking care of my family and tried my best to make sure they were happy. I was extremely good at staying busy, taking care of everyone else's needs, so I didn't have to look at how miserable I had become. Wasn't that clever? I knew I was drowning but I just didn't have the strength, courage or energy to do anything to help myself at that point. I was way beyond burnout. All the avoidance had me pinching off my life force to the point of exhaustion and overwhelm.

I didn't even stop to think if anyone could help me!

The thought of being alone, divorced and struggling kept me stuck in my comfort zone. I was being taken care of and I didn't have to work. I dreaded the thought of what my life would be like if I left. I had been through a divorce before and divorce meant suffering to me. I felt I was already at the bottom of the rabbit hole and was petrified to sink any lower. I was not a spring chicken and the thought of starting over again had me frozen in fear, yet I knew I had to do something, soon.

It was time to reach out.

I had a close friend that I went out with occasionally, for some much-needed girls-night-out time. I began sharing my stories with her, crying and complaining at how miserable I was. She gave me multiple gentle nudges that it was time to get out of my comfort zone. She had me think about my responsibility in all of this and said it is time to change my circumstances. I had to get back in touch with me and look at all the areas I had been avoiding. With my friends help, I started taking small steps that helped me get stronger and build my confidence. A renewed spark began to ignite within me.

It was as if I had popped the cork off a champagne bottle and all of me that was pent up exploded out. It was time to own my voice and speak the hell up. I wasn't holding back anymore. Now I could feel the wide range of emotions that I had been scared to face. Dammit! It was about damn time and it sure felt exhilarating. I felt ALIVE!

I finally felt confident and strong enough to have a much-needed conversation with my partner. I told him I wanted him to sit and listen until I was done. I didn't care about the outcome after our conversation. I had accepted that if he wanted out of the relationship after our talk, that was okay with me. He was non-responsive to the conversation. This wasn't about him. This was about me. I owned my voice finally, since that summer night when I was seven years old.

I took ownership of my life, my choices and what I wanted just for me.

I wasn't trying to escape my pain or avoid confrontational situations. I was no longer a victim of my past. I made a decision that something had to change, so I sought help. I began working with coaches and I began putting the pieces together. I was not feeling the full range of senses within my body. I wasn't aware that other people had different sensations than those who have experienced sexual and emotional trauma. I could feel hot and cold but not the depth of sensations that are available to experience. I didn't even know how to explain it because there was no awareness, at that time.

I worked with skilled somatic massage therapists on deep levels of self-introspection and self-healing. I began listening to my body and opening up to a plethora of new sensations.

It was during my career as a massage therapist that I deepened my knowledge of touch and how the body's sensations are always telling us something. About how emotions get stored in our tissue, our cells.

I had now gained sovereignty over my life.

Sovereignty is the full right and power of a governing body over itself, without any interference from outside sources or bodies.

I gave myself permission to choose what was right for me and what felt good. I would no longer base my decisions on how they would affect others or if I was going to hurt someone else's feelings. Now as harsh as that sounds, I took baby steps to reclaim ownership of my life. I learned to say no without guilt. Over time it became easier and it felt really good to do so.

I felt my power being restored. It was like a huge weight was lifted. All my years of blaming him, complaining about how miserable I was and it was all gone. I could breathe deeply again. I was free at last. My life transformed.

This new chapter brought a spark of life back to my once dull body and spirit.

My story is filled with broken pieces, terrible choices and ugly truths, I had to face. It's also filled with my amazing comeback, peace in my heart and grace that saved my life, beyond what I once imagined.

In the past, as one of my ugly habits, I used my looks and my sex appeal to get what I wanted. Now I have learned that there is a flowing well within me that is always working on my behalf. My body is the temple that my soul resides in and it is up to me to keep it tuned in, turned on and turned up to a higher frequency.

The more vibrant I began to feel, the more I learned to lean in and listen to my body's wisdom. I had tapped into an energy frequency that nurtured me, nourished me and made me feel loved.

We all have our experiences of early trauma, whether consciously or unconsciously. We learned to give away our power to others, instead of honoring the choices that felt right. It became the way we operated in our world. Rules become something we automatically adhere to; deference to authority becomes natural and doing as your told becomes a standard default mode running your subconscious in the background. We are not even aware of it happening.

In the process of pursuing my dreams, there were various hardships. The struggle was real. There were moments when I didn't have food to feed my children, or gas to get home, and even times when I wanted to simply give up and go back. But I didn't go back, because I didn't want to pass on the weight of settling and compromising in ways I previously had, to my daughters.

The decision to clear the clutter from my path and to regain sight of who I truly am is completely within making our own choices. It's been my mission for many years. Now I am able to help other women who passionately desire the freedom to be who they are.

Gaining one's sovereignty is to have full freedom of expression, and freedom to become consciously aware of one's authentic self, rather than being strapped down by the expectations of everyone else's beliefs and desires.

You too can find what fuels your passion towards your own authenticity, the real reclaiming of your true self. For it is THAT person who came to live in this world, and that person we need to create a more authentic world to live in.

"I was raised to sense
what someone wanted me
to be and be that
kind of person.
It took me a long time
not to judge myself through
someone else's eyes."

— Sally Field

Christine Cattogio

Christine is an Internationally Recognized Life Transition Strategist and Women's Empowerment Coach.

She specializes in helping women Reawaken, Refine and Redesign their life. Her programs are designed to teach women to rise above life's challenges and transform into the best version of themselves into the life they truly desire and deserve.

A sought after Certified speaker, she has been a keynote presenter for both live events and radio platforms. She is a contributing author in the International Best Sellers *"Bold is Beautiful"* and *"Bold is Beautiful - Breakthrough to Business Strategies"*.

www.Christinecatoggio.com

Chapter Ten

The Power Within

Christine Catoggio

We had been waiting for this day for over 2 years. Like a bad dream, we were hoping it would never come to pass. Yet, there we were, on a grey, overcast Fall morning, in a strange town, knowing that, in a few short minutes, we would be saying farewell to the perfect, fairy tale life we had come to know and stepping in to a world far removed from anything we could ever have imagined.

As I looked across the car as he drove, on this seemingly endless highway, I felt sorry for him. I knew that he was scared. I was scared too!

I wanted to scream out at him "I hate you for allowing this to happen to our family!" I felt hurt, betrayed, and angry! How could he leave me like this? How could he have made choices and decisions that affected our whole family, without consulting me? What had made him veer off the course that we had planned for our lives?

As I watched him, hunched and cowering, walk through the doors of the Federal Penitentiary, I was numb. Numb with fear for me and for him. I felt sheer terror watching him walk away and could hardly imagine what he must have been feeling, his tough exterior now diminished to a terrified, frightened shell of a man. A shiver ran down my spine – I wasn't sure if it was the raw, damp air, or an emotional shock wave, but it was like nothing that I had ever felt before.

I remember driving to the beach, knowing I had a few hours before my flight left to take me back home. The beach was eerily quiet, which seemed to magnify my overwhelming sense of aloneness. I parked the car in the empty lot and lingered in my aloneness. I wanted to weep, but the tears would not flow. I stared at the ocean, mesmerized by how easily the waves ebbed and flowed – almost trance like. I'm not sure if I dozed off or if I was hypnotized by the waves, but, for a few short minutes, I felt almost out of body, as though I was watching myself lull into rest.

We had been married for 25 years. Everything about my life included him. We had so many dreams and plans for our life. A lifetime of shared goals, now gone awry. How was I going to survive without him? What were my next steps? I wasn't used to being alone. I have never had to do life alone! The thought of spending the next three years of his incarceration alone, was sheer terror for me.

I had been young and naive when we married. I was the proverbial "good girl" – Daddy's little girl. I always followed the rules and did everything that was expected of me. My father was a strong presence in my life. He was loving and supportive, but strong and commanding in a "Father Knows Best" sort of way. He was a police officer in a day when that role alone commanded respect and obedience. And, as the little girl, the daughter of a police officer with a strong Italian upbringing, I learned at a young age to do what I was told to do, never answer back, and "children should be seen, and not heard." I grew up with a powerful rule book that had no room for imperfection.

And now this perfect life that I had worked so hard to create had imploded before my very eyes! How will we ever recover from this? How will "I" ever be able to put Humpty Dumpty back together again?

How will I ever be able to pick up the pieces of my shattered world, and function normally again?

I was so overwhelmed. As I watched the ebb and flow of the ocean, I started to sob uncontrollably. Life as I knew it would never be the same. My world was shattered! Rocked!

My flight was delayed and didn't land until 1:00AM. Getting off the airplane, alone, in a totally deserted airport, was terrifying. I felt vulnerable and frightened as I walked through the empty airport toward the parking garage. I don't ever recall feeling so terrified in my life. I could not get home fast enough and pull the covers over my head. I wanted to hide. Hide from the world, and the horror that was now my life.

Surprisingly, I slept soundly through the rest of the night.

The next morning, I was abruptly awakened by the incessant ringing of my phone. I could hear my daughters making a lot of commotion in the family room. As I jumped out of bed to scream at them to quiet down and leave me alone, they were rushing in, hysterical, crying and calling out to me.

It was the morning of September 11th, 2001.

As I watched the horrific events of that day unfold before my eyes, I froze. I couldn't feel anything! I couldn't cry. All I could do was stare at the horror unfolding before my eyes. I felt as though the blood had been drained from my body, and rigor mortise had set in. I felt dead. Everything that I knew, everything that I believed to be safe and secure, had been shattered. The unbelievable events, the things that were once only real in movies, were now real. This nightmare cannot be my life! I wanted to wake up from this horrific dream, but there was no escaping it. I was the lead role in the most horrific scenario – my life!

It was an excruciating first year. I experienced all the stages of grief, and then some. I was angry. I was sad. I was lonely. I missed his presence. I missed having him to talk to. I needed his advice. How do I pay these bills? What do I do about the house, the girls? It was hard to cram all that in a 3-minute conversation, once a week, over the phone. I struggled through so many difficult challenges that my head was spinning.

About 6 months had passed. One gorgeous day I decided to clear my head and go to the beach. I needed to get away, to escape the bills that were piling up, the endless chores that were waiting for my attention, and the walls that seemed to be closing in on me. I knew I had to make a decision.

I hadn't been going out much. I had become somewhat of a recluse. I remember feeling as though I had a big "A" on my chest (a reference to the book "Scarlet Letter"). Many of my so called "friends" knew what had happened. It was very publicized, and in a small-town word can travel quickly. It was never discussed openly, but I couldn't help noticing the whispers that stopped when I walked into a room, and the invitations that waned.

The beach was so freeing. It felt good to be out in the open. Taking in the crisp salt air, the wind flowing through my hair, seemed to energize me. I was starting to feel alive again. I remember feeling the warm ocean water enveloping me, soothing me as though it was wrapping me in a comforting embrace. I closed my eyes and allowed the waves to carry me as though I was on a cloud. It was mesmerized, trance like, and my mind seemed to wander in a space I had never felt before. "Just one wave" I thought, "and it will be all over."

Suddenly, I was jolted awake as the waves quickly released me, and I began to sob. I realized how close I had come to ending my misery and my life!

I was startled. What was I thinking? I have so much to live for. I am stronger than this! I'm not ready to give up!

At that moment, I made a decision to fight the demons that had been attacking me and to take charge of my own life. I was responsible for my life. I knew that I had a lot of work to do to find my way back to the woman I was meant to be, and I knew, at that moment, that I was ready to take my power back and not be a victim to my circumstances any longer. I knew that God had saved me in that moment. That he wasn't done with me yet, and I had so much more to do. I suddenly felt a surge of strength that I had not experienced in many months.

The next morning, I opened the drapes and let the sun in for the first time in quite a while. I sat down at my desk and decided to confront the pile of bills that were staring at me every morning, robbing me of my confidence and self-worth.

One by one, I picked up the phone and addressed the glaring balances that I had been avoiding. I realized that avoidance was making me feel weak and powerless. With every call that I made, I started feeling a little bit stronger. I was no longer a pathetic scofflaw, avoiding the bills that I owed, but a strong woman taking charge of her circumstances, and taking back control of my life. It gave me a sense of freedom. I started to feel stronger and more confident. I envisioned myself in a Super Woman outfit, and when "stuff" came at me, I deflected it with golden cuffs!

Slowly but surely, parts of me that were lost, began to resurface. I was terrified of falling back into the rabbit hole, so I created rituals for reinforcement. I knew that I needed to build my muscles again. My mental muscle, to keep me in fight, not flight mode. I needed to confront my fears, and angst, and do the work that would bring me back to the woman I once was.

I knew that there was a lesson through everything I had been through and I started to do the work on myself that would help me heal.

There were so many parts of me that needed to heal. It was like peeling an onion. Where do I begin?

I began to journal at night before I went to bed. It allowed me to release any angst and pent up emotions of the day. It also helped me to get very clear on where my pain was, what direction I needed to move to heal next, and allowed me to acknowledge, and be grateful for all the good that was happening in my life. I realized that making this decision and gaining clarity was what I needed to move forward.

As I started to get more clarity and direction, I felt stronger. Emotionally stronger, but physically neglected. I had not been taking care of myself. Stress played a major role, but I also wasn't eating properly. I had little or no appetite, was running my butt off trying to get my business up and running, and basically neglecting "me".

Eventually, it took its toll. I was running out to an early morning network meeting, and I got delayed.

My stomach was doing some strange things, and I couldn't leave the house for a while. I was confined to the bathroom! When I got to the meeting, I shared with a friend what had happened. Of course, she advised me to get to a doctor. As the meeting was ending, I went to stand up, and collapsed to the floor. What I hadn't shared was that this had been happening for a few days. She rushed me to the emergency room, and I ended up being admitted with ulcerative colitis.

The next few days in the hospital gave me the opportunity to evaluate all the areas of my life that I had been neglecting. I made a promise to myself that if I ever wanted to take my power back, I needed to take care of me first. Taking care of everyone else first had almost cost me my life!

It was time for me to heal. Heal the pain of the hurt I had felt, the pain of abandonment I felt from my life partner. The pain of feeling displaced from the world I had been comfortable in and thrust into an unknown world. That dark, squirmy, icky chrysalis place, feeling confined, and ready to break through!

Now, it was time for me to rise up and be the butterfly. Fly!

I began to strategize my comeback. I needed to get my physical strength back. Out of necessity at first, I began a healthy diet regimen. When I was feeling stronger, I began walking every morning. Not only did it clear my mind, it energized my body.

So began my breakthrough. I no longer felt powerless and weak, I felt strong and empowered. Energizing my body energized my mind. The cobwebs were cleared.

What a process of self-discovery! I realized that through my life, I didn't really know who "I" was. I was busy being who everyone else wanted me to be. I was a daughter, a sister, a wife and a mother, but I never truly learned who Christine was.

And now I had a blank slate, to discover who I was at my core.

I was startled awake one night, with a divine download - "reclaim inner soul energy." I spent hours in the darkness, searching for the meaning. What does it really mean to reclaim inner soul energy?

Reclaim — Take back the part of you — Inner Soul — that has been hidden away – Energy — denying you from who you are meant to be. It even had an acronym - R.I.S.E. It is a process of healing the heart and soul, discovering and defining your own core values, and developing self-awareness of your own purpose and fulfillment.

Once I began to R.I.S.E. and harness the power within, there was no stopping me. I began mentoring other women who are stuck the way I had been. I knew that through my experiences, I could help other women who were trying to find their way back from life's traumas. I had the tools. I acknowledged how powerful I truly am. If I could guide one woman at a time through the chrysalis, then I have found my purpose.

I was always a student of the Wizard of Oz, because of all the metaphors of women's empowerment in the story. A good friend who had witnessed my metamorphosis sent me a gift of a Ruby Slipper lapel pin. I wore it proudly, as a badge of honor, as a reminder that I've had the power all along. I have the Power! The power to create whatever I set my mind to.

The power is in all of us. Surrendering to it is freeing! Once you can walk through the fears and be open to the Divine Guidance that is supporting you, anything is possible.

Allow the Power Within to lead you to the life that you are destined to live.

"The Goddess doesn't enter us from outside; she emerges from deep within. She is not held back by what happened in the past. She is conceived in consciousness, born in love, and nurtured by higher thinking. She is integrity and value, created and sustained by the hard work of personal growth and the discipline of a life lived actively in hope."

~ Marianne Williamson

"*You've been criticizing
yourself for years
and it hasn't worked.
Try approving of yourself
and see what happens.*"

~ Louise Hay

Angela Jones-Taul

Angela Jones Taul is an LPN and a licensed Massage Therapist. She is the owner of Pure Touch Massage Center in Maysville, Kentucky. An active participant in her church community, Angela leads a women's open share group and also a 12-step study group for the Celebrate Recovery Ministry. Resonating with a Goddess mentality helped her find her inner beauty, light and strength. Angela has a strong desire to be an inspirational voice for girls, young ladies and women of all cultures. Look for her debut book to be released in the Spring of 2020.

Email Angela at angelashines@yahoo.com

Chapter Eleven

Whispers from an Angel

Angela Jones-Taul

When I was born an angel whispered to me,

"The essence of your soul is locked with a key.

You hold the access deep within and
you won't immediately see

What your light is meant to be."

As my light began to shine within,

The world would introduce me to sin.

A loss of innocence and burdened with shame,

My light became dim and I took the blame.

Too much for my young mind to bear

I became lost, feeling like no one cared.

The dark shadows are what appealed to me now.

My inner voice, Esther, would reign with her crown,

Spending years developing a mask that could hide

The raging battle going on in my mind.

Once again, my angel whispered in my ear,

"Keep shining your light and dry up those tears."

I felt a wave of redeeming grace

Knowing this wasn't the end of my race.

My light began to brighten my soul.

The darkness would fight to gain control.

This time it would deliver a devastating blow

To punish my growth and dim my glow.

I wanted to end this torturous game.

I attempted to extinguish my beautiful flame.

My angel would appear once again,

Not to whisper but to proclaim,

"If you don't own your gifts from within

I have no choice but to let the darkness win.

Ignite your flame and shine it bright,

Your inner beauty has always been the light.

Balance your light with the dark,

Embracing Esther is where you start.

Give her love and she will see

That your purpose will bring you peace."

No longer relating to the negative words

Unworthy, unloved and even unclean.

Shed your mask and add some vulnerability,

You have a new name to claim and positive energy.

Let's start with loved, worthy and enough.

Add courageous and independent, girl strut your stuff!

I love who I am, this is me,

An emerging Goddess

So it is, so it be.

My angel came once again and whispered to me,

"You've always had a purpose.

I just needed you to see

What an amazing woman you turned out to be."

Growing up in a small town in Kentucky, I had no understanding of how important self-love was or even how to achieve this crucial tool to keep my sanity. The search for love and acceptance kept me looking in all the wrong places, instead of within myself. It made me a target for manipulative behaviors from others that I didn't recognize as a young girl. I was accepting less than what I deserved because I had no idea of my self-worth. I became a people pleaser, a codependent woman. I developed a victim mentality and as a sensitive empath, one who can feel others pain, I had no idea that my happiness was not to be in found in others.

When my soul awakened to heal the wounds I encountered early in life, I regained my identity and no longer needed approval from society. The reflection I had seen in the mirror, which used to be my worst enemy, now became a reflection of the goddess within. I removed the mask I used to hide behind and the pain began to dissipate. I was learning how to love myself and be proud of the woman I am.

One day I made a decision and said yes to coaching. This process helped me identify parts of myself I was not even aware of; like the victim mentality and how strongly I was holding onto it. I was in shock when I first realized this, never imagining that I was not living in 100% gratitude. I was actually upset at first and triggered, to be honest. How did I become a constant complainer? Why was I focusing always on the bad things in life? My coach supported me through this process and my sabotaging voice, named Esther, my inner child soon became my powerhouse. I realized my younger self was that voice and she kept me in a 'comfort zone', to survive. She protected me and limited me.

We were both afraid to move forward because we didn't know how to take the first steps. I needed to embrace Esther, talk to her, appreciate her and love her. It may sound bizarre and crazy, but it helped me immensely.

The beauty of acknowledging Esther helped me to identify and begin to accept who I am. I no longer avoid understanding my hurts and hang ups. I learned what it meant to be codependent and accepting the truth of the meaning spoke volumes. Being codependent means you support or enable another individual's manipulative, controlling behaviors. You need their approval or validation. You compromise values, choices, and personal well-being to be accepted. You lose sight of who you really are to gain their attention and what you think is love. Codependency was the way I was seeking love and approval and I made another decision to heal.

That dark day came when I wanted to end my life. Yes, me! Strong and independent I could not handle my life anymore. This was crazy! However, it was my breaking and turning point to propel change.

I began seeking for non-traditional ways to help, alongside professional help. I attended small women's groups at church, personal coaching sessions that also had private mastermind groups; where like-minded individuals desiring to achieve wholeness and a better life would support each other's growth.

It all helped to fuel my own process of wanting more. When you begin listening to your heart and check the "ego", your self-reflection becomes more noticeable and you start to discover who you are deep inside. This personal growth and maturity have fueled a passion for living my best life. I am a goddess arising and emerging into her purpose. I have chosen to let go of the past hurts and victim mentality. I am victorious! Now I am stepping out of limited beliefs to pursue my dreams.

Potential and Purpose

Potential and purpose dwell in my soul,

My Goddess colors - purple, green and glorious gold!

An empowered woman who will help fix your crown

'Cause potential and purpose is what I have found.

No longer denying but accepting my worth,

Please honor my rebirth.

Love, beauty, confidence in check,

Full Goddess mode in effect,

Motivating and inspiration are my goals.

For all women sparkle, some just don't know

They have potential and purpose hidden deep within.

Positive encouragement will help them win.

I build my tribe with powerful women

The ones whose hearts are full of giving,

Role models to all with their service.

All women have potential and purpose.

Our outreach is for the young and seasoned,

This is from our heart, no other reason.

Women coming together as one.

Potential and purpose have begun.

*"You and I possess
within ourselves at every
moment of our lives,
under all circumstances,
the power to transform the
quality of our lives."*

– Werner Erhard

Gloria Coppola

Gloria Coppola - author, visionary, spiritual coach, retreat leader, creative writing coach, empath and publisher. Gloria has spent decades serving in the healing arts, as a former owner of a holistic center, massage school and health food store. She is an award-winning international educator, her legacy and contribution hold her in high regard in the Massage Hall of Fame and she was recognized as a humanitarian for helping colleagues after a hurricane. Gloria's devotion to service and helping resides within her at a cellular level. Through her coaching she helps others understand their soul purpose journey. Gloria has been a featured writer for over four decades in multiple books, holistic magazines, newspapers and is the proud publisher of this coauthored book.

Totally driven by her intuition and faith, she has forged through many tragic life events, all guiding her to greater purpose and inner peace. Her greatest desire is to help others learn to trust their process and reach their full potential.

Contact Gloria to schedule coaching, publish a book or to book a soul purpose consultation email gloria@gloriacoppola.com

www.gloriacoppola.com
www.powerfulpotentialandpurpose.com
https://www.facebook.com/soulFULLpurpose
https://www.facebook.com/unlockyoursoulpotential/

Chapter Twelve

Shattered Pieces

Gloria Coppola

"Daring greatly means the courage to be vulnerable. It means to show up and be seen, to ask for what you need, to talk about how you're feeling, to have the hard conversations."

~ Brené Brown

Those big blues eyes that captured every heart and soul and those round chubby cheeks she wore so rosy, always had a sense of wonder. Little would this five-year-old know that the mosaic brooch of her mom's that caught her fancy would become a spiritual symbol of her life. It signified the various patterns in which we live. These delicate shattered pieces of glass were about to teach her more than she could ever dream in that imaginative mind she had or the wild thoughts no one ever understood.

Her golden-brown locks of banana curls would bounce like Tigger when she joyfully skipped across the cold, hard, tiled floor. It was a long hallway. As she pushed open the door to her parents' room with a sense of adventure, like Dorothy in the wizard of Oz, it was even more exciting each time. Her curiosity got the best of her imagination as she would think, "What magic would be revealed to her today?"

The long, sheer, white chiffon curtains would blow in the cool spring breeze through the old window frame, although she imagined them to be angels' wings. She frolicked through them and let them gently caress her face, almost like it was a kiss from the angels. She would pause, smile and feel blessed by God. She took a quick moment to quietly peek over her shoulder, to make sure she was alone. She walked past the massive bed her parents slept in as she moved cautiously, tiptoeing towards that magical box that always piqued her curiosity.

It seemed to have a magical pull, an unstoppable calling to examine it more closely, every time she held it in her hand.

Her imagination always danced in her head, like colorful fairies. Each time she was going to lift open that magical box, she hoped to see something elegant, something exciting and perhaps something for a princess to wear, or a treasure of gold.

Ever so gently her tiny, chubby fingers would touch the lid of her mom's jewelry box, admiring the mother of pearl oriental motif. It seemed to glitter as the sun would shine upon it, each color magically swirling before her eyes. In her mind's eye she would see princesses dancing on a beach. Somehow, she just seemed to know her thoughts could make things happen. Often, she would get sidetracked dancing like a ballerina. Then slipping her hand into the pretty velvet bag, she gently pulled it out. She didn't want to get caught holding the raised pieces of glass that delicately created the daisies, roses and other little flowers. She was very careful! The colorful enamel piece of jewelry was her treasure and she never wanted anything to happen to it.

She never really understood her intense curiosity, but one day her vivid imagination would prove to be a great insight on this journey of life. She would discover her true gift. You are about to learn how this insight - her intuition and curiosity - will take her to places she never knew she would visit. You will gain insight along this journey with her as one day she finds what she was looking for. And one day she would learn how these shattered pieces of glass would change her life, forever.

Forty years later during her favorite time of the year, Christmas, she would place a beautiful porcelain angel in the foyer of her new home. The sun was shining like rays from heaven as rainbow colors flashed through onto the walls in the hall, making everything glitter. She felt that same presence, as she recalled on those days when she was five. She remembered, out of nowhere, how shattered broken pieces of glass could create such a beautiful bouquet of flowers.

When her mom passed, she was 18. The mosaic brooch was the only thing she had requested from her dad. It was a reminder of the magic and love that exists in one's heart. Now this love was with her once again in this one moment in time.

It was time to decorate the Christmas tree in her new house with her husband. Six months ago, their wedding was on the beach with beautiful princesses dancing all dressed in rainbow colors, just as she had imagined many years prior. It was a joyful day, one where everyone got to play and call upon that magical space to experience a joyful union.

Christmas brought a childlike joy to every cell in her body, like blowing bubbles in the summer breezes. She sang Christmas carols like "O Holy Night" and pretended to be the angel Gloria as she rejoiced in the memories of growing up in an Italian family.

The next day something beyond her imagination would change the course of her life and enhance her intuitive gifts that she often hid.

It had been a very hectic week, as one can imagine. Baking cookies, cleaning house, working, wrapping presents and feeling overwhelmed with so many things happening for so many people. Her empathic skills and highly sensitive connection to others was at a peak for some reason and she could feel something was wrong, big time. After a long day at work, too tired to think, exhausted and wishing someone would make her dinner tonight, she walked into the beautiful foyer and the porcelain angel seemed to assure her, "Everything will be okay." Later that evening, she would write in her journal, giving gratitude as she had for many years and ending it with, "I just want peace."

She would awaken early the next day, to prepare for Christmas Eve coming up. Being very methodical in those days and anal about cleaning, she got down on her hands and knees to wash the brand-new sparkling tiles in the foyer. After all, the new in-law family was coming over and she had to make everything glow. Her perfectionism with detail consumed her mind, remembering how her father would always want the best from her in all situations.

Suddenly she heard a big thump from the upstairs master bedroom. Gazing with her tired blue eyes she looked up the stairs to see her husband stumbling down them as if he was drunk. He had a look of rage in his eyes, blood shot, disoriented and saying words unrecognizable. The night prior he didn't feel well and had flu like symptoms, so she got up off the floor to help him when he stumbled over her to grab his car keys.

Just then those eyes, like a demon, looked deep into her soft blue eyes, piercing, snidely smiling before he turned and threw the brand-new birthday watch she had gifted him a few weeks prior. The demon, she thought, was the one he talked about when struggling with his opioid addiction. She was terrified and could not move. Nothing but an endless silence that felt like eternity. She slipped away, feeling very young and lost, very scared and just watched him walking towards the front door.

Her beautiful angel, Oh NO! The shattered pieces sprinkling through the ray of light left her stunned as he walked out the door. A gut-wrenching scream welled up from the depths of her soul and a massive energy rose staring into the eyes of the demon as he kicked the angel and then slammed the door and walked away.

Yes, I was the little girl and now everything was going to shift. My intuition was proving to be spot on. My heart was pounding, my soul was reassuring me, yet something was off, something was different and something else was telling me in a quiet stillness, "It's all an illusion."

Eight days would go by, like an eternity, my heart feeling broken. I felt as if I was in the picture framed over my couch, caught in a dimension that seemed parallel. I could see everything from a new perspective, yet I felt numb. I recalled the words from a priest when I was 12, when he said to me "Everything, my child, has a purpose."

The nights were endless, dark, the winds howling. Sunrises and sunsets rolled into another. Unable to close those beautiful blues, lying awake, wondering, praying and feeling distraught, not knowing where he was. Help came from my colleagues and students, friends and family, as the days got more frigid with blizzard-like storm conditions. Snow fell harder across the fields and in the parks, Christmas trees lit on front lawns twinkled as we searched with slippery, icy roads, when I felt "it".

You know that "IT" when something doesn't feel right, or good, or when you just know something has shifted, something's different and the energy you once knew has transmuted and ascended.

Someone knocked at the door as my mind wandered away. Time stood still for a moment, because there was that knowing again. In walked a rookie cop, giving me the news.

"NO!!!!!!" The scream was gut-wrenching as I slammed my fist so hard on the cold counter top, it's amazing I didn't break it.

I passed out momentarily when I heard the words "found buried beneath the fallen snow" after a somber Christmas day had passed. The gifts still lay unopened under the Christmas tree. The meaning of Christmas would never be the same. Now as I watch people spend thriftlessly each year, putting themselves into debt, or never even reaching out to loved ones they haven't seen in years I think of this moment. It can all be taken away in the blink of an eye and what is left only exists in the heart.

Time stood still and yet it flew by. I could not explain the existence I was living in. Dreams were heightened and my husband would visit me, so why was I planning a funeral? Friends came by and I went through the motions. You know, where people expect you to be okay, so you are, and it makes them feel better.

It ended. My life as I knew it ended. The goals all accomplished now had no meaning. The years of building a lasting relationship were an illusion. The sense of success meant nothing. The control over things I thought I could create, nothing, no meaning, only a choice how I would deal or not.

Months went by and I had absolutely no desire to get out of the bed, to go to work or teach my students. I wanted to die too, as nothing seemed to have meaning or purpose any longer. The only thing I remember was my daughter saying, "Mom, you take as long as you need." So, I did.

Eventually the depression sunk so deep I didn't know if I could find my way out, or if I even wanted to because it actually felt safer in there, if that makes sense. My intuition was heightening more than ever, and my senses were inexplicably high in altered realities. It was overwhelming at times! Was I really going in and out of realms of consciousness, hallucinating even though I was on no medications? Or was I just merely insane or simply dreaming? Perhaps this is the awakening some speak about; I had no idea.

It didn't feel like an awakening, however it was definitely a dark night of the soul.

The insanity continued as paranormal phenomena happened around me daily. How could this be? Objects being moved, messages being found, dreams feeling like I was in an altered reality. Have you ever felt your loved one so close, even though they were gone? Have you felt as if you were going crazy because synchronicities were so frequent that you didn't believe it to be true?

I was blessed to have a counselor who understood this heightened sense and encouraged me to stay connected to the communication I was having with the loss of my beloved soul mate. Then one day I couldn't take it anymore. It was too intense. Again, that energy rose in my belly and I screamed, "STOP!" It got quiet in my mind and in my house after that, no signs anywhere for months upon months. What had I done? I began searching more. For what, I didn't know just then. An answer, an insight, a solution? I was missing something but I could not explain it.

"Perhaps I will sell my home and all the possessions and just leave?" Perhaps there was something out there for me to learn, to be, to see, to know, that shook me up to see possibilities in other worlds of existence? Perhaps all the losses I had gone through were to find something deeper inside me, a truth I had yet to uncover. Was there a treasure waiting, like the one I had been seeking since I opened that magical box at five years old? I had to trust this innate "knowing" and trust my inner voice leading me to unknown places, to leave everything that I knew; my business, friends and family. What the hell was I doing?

Paulo Coelho, the alchemist states, "This is why alchemy exists, so that everyone will search for his treasure, find it and then want to be better than he was in his former life.

The element of lead will play its role until the world has no further need for lead; and then lead will have to turn itself into gold. That's what alchemists do. They show that when we strive to become better than we are, everything around us becomes better too."

Intuition is one of our greatest birthrights and treasures gifted to us. When we make the decision to trust it and combine the energy within us with everything around us, we can transform to our higher selves and take our journey to another level of consciousness. Was this my path and purpose? I was about to explore and find out. Was I so brainwashed, previously operating mostly from the conditioned linear mind, that I forgot who I was? Did I really have doctrines so heavily ingrained in my subconscious that I lost sight of what is truly important?

The decision was made, by chance, by synchronicity, making no sense to many.

There I was getting in my car when a young boy ran over

to me and asked, "Miss, are you leaving all this stuff for the garbage, even the new stuff in boxes?"

"Yes," I told him, as I drove away with a sense of no attachment to anything, feeling disconnected, still numb, anxious and unsure. The only thing I knew was I had to go. Off I went on my own "Eat, Pray, Love" journey two decades ago. Egypt, Hawaii and Peru.

"She's got the life." I heard the whispers, I knew. "Look at her living in Kauai and leaving everything behind. How could she do that?" The whispers got louder in my head and then I released them. Just like that! I was not going to play that game in my head. I could not, because my life depended on it and not guilt, shame, judgement or old beliefs were going to stop the exploration I was about to go on for my soul purpose.

You see, I would learn something profound, and it would help me help others in the future. But until I could release the old voices in my head and transmute the life I knew, into the life I was meant to live, I would stay stuck in this prison in my mind. I made one decision to say "YES!" to be guided intuitively. I have not stopped since that day.

I was on a journey of truth, of spiritual peace. As my Hawaiian mentor would say, Pono.

I experienced initiations in Peru with shaman that would provide me greater insight and open my 6th chakra, or 3rd eye as some know it, to more vision and insights. I studied with kahuna about the deeper connection with the divine feminine, Mother Earth and learned how to create the balance in life that is so necessary to reach higher states of energy, of consciousness, naturally. I experienced a dimensional shift in the Great Pyramid on a full blue moon, after chanting with twelve others, when my deceased mother would show up to talk to me and tell me it was time to live my life.

All of these experiences shifted my energy to levels I had never experienced. I truly felt I could fly. I had no fear!

My thirst for knowledge exploded. My curiosity came back like that child once again. I woke up joyful, with a simple life and way of living. I connected with mother nature and all the internal forces that aligned me with her as my healing went deeper. I would continue to expand my senses; my inner knowledge and my soul wisdom were awakening. While I cannot explain it all in words, I can tell you the feeling was like a shell coming off my body. Like a vice grip being released from my brain, a blindfold over my eyes removed, the deep sense of peace I had asked for that last evening in my journal came to me. Yes Peace! That deep sense that provides you a space to observe, to know, to live in your truth and follow your soul wisdom. A deeper sense to guide you through this journey if you are willing to pay attention. I did not realize how important spiritual peace would be in the future years when people would not understand, when they could not hear my truth and they did not understand my honesty.

I remember reading several articles and books years later describing spiritual alchemy as a freeing of one's spiritual self, the one which is trapped in fears, beliefs, lack of worthiness, etc. Spiritual alchemy became the way to release my core wounds and beliefs, to reconnect with my soul in order to live more freely from within, to limit and eliminate self-destructive behaviors. I found my own core values. For me it became the existence of feeling free and unobstructed to exist in a natural state of peace. The pure, soulful awareness, the gold, the treasure in the magic box. The pieces of being whole, once again.

Carl Jung wrote "I had a series of dreams which dealt with the same theme." In 1926 Jung dreamed himself into being captive in the 17th century. Not much later, he says, did he realize that the dream referred to alchemy and that alchemy is a symbolic representation of the individuation process of transformation. At five years old, I had a series of the same dream for weeks and those same dreams would show up again later in life. It was all symbolic and while I had no clue as a child, I always remembered it. Yes, I would know what it meant.

I began to recall many studies during my life from Jung, along with many other meta-physicians, spiritual leaders, authors. Always inquisitive, at a very young age I began learning a variety of sciences, beliefs and insights. I recalled that conversation with the priest at the age of 12, once again, where he told me to seek the truth, to study religion, philosophy, metaphysics and go back in time to learn more about the ancient ways.

My path and purpose were being guided all the time, from the very beginning. All the symbols and signs showing me the way. Did it mean I wasn't insane after all; but listening deeply to a wisdom of understanding that would open channels?

Eventually, I would come to learn about Magnum Opus, the individuation process in Jungian psychology whereby an individual realizes a state of spiritual and psychological wholeness. Through this process what was previously fragmented and broken is restored and synthesized so we are whole, our uniqueness emerges, and we fully embrace our authentic destiny. This is our movement away from what I call the linear brainwashing or the pawn in society to a consciously collaborating self-realization in one's unique soul purpose. We begin to see life more symbolically and are led from this soul consciousness to a greater sense of self.

The guidance I was continually shown in life, from that first sense of angels kissing me and the symbolism of the shattered pieces in that magical box, to the moment the porcelain angel was shattered by the dark side, has opened me to see with new perspective on all of life. It has helped me cope with other life lessons and helped me be more forgiving of myself and others. This soul alchemy has provided greater insight to follow my intuition and guides me to all the right people, places, situations, circumstances, resources and finances in life that help me serve at a higher level, to continue becoming the best version of myself on this life journey.

Is it easy? Hell no!

However, looking back over the six decades from my most vivid memories, I totally understand how we are all being shown the way, if we just pay attention. Our soul is always trying to show us what we need but often we over-analyze and don't trust. We make our excuses out of fear, scarcity, we listen to other people, we follow the crowd and limit our thinking and our potential.

I can tell you my heightened inner senses have taken me to places I never imagined I would go and introduced me to many people that have helped me along the way. I can tell you making that one decision to trust my birth right gift of intuition has helped me, and others, on multiple levels. I can tell you that the magic of that five-year-old girl is ever emerging in curiosity, more each day, about all the secret treasures of life. I can tell you I feel fully blessed by the angels each day and that knowing and living in my truth is the best feeling I can wake up with each day, in full gratitude.

The blue-eyed angel lives in me each day. Her name was given in honor of the angel in the highest, the one that sits next to God. Gloria. I now honor this gift, this wisdom, this position and I continue to ask for guidance to serve at my highest each day. I may not have liked all my life challenges, all the losses, pain and lessons; however, I've seen worse for those that remain prisoners in their own suffering, limiting their potential. It is my prayer that each person wakes up to the magic and lives their authentic self from the soul level, to be all they can be in this world. Each of us is needed to make the positive changes in the lives of our fellow earthlings.

Oh, the stories we tell ourselves, the journeys we experience, the life adventures we take. All unravel in time to show us the beauty within each of us and what we can create.

Creating this coauthored book is like that mosaic, putting all the pieces of these brave and courageous women together! I never imagined this would be my journey now. However, I recall as I write this, that I was the literary editor of my high school magazine. It was all in the plan. Your soul knows.

Imagine the places you will go. (Dr. Seuss) when you trust your inner senses.

Just like the moon we all wax and wane.
There are times we live in the shadows of darkness,
Where no one looks for us or even seems to care if we are here.

A glimpse of our light may peek out beyond the ships,
hoping that the smile in the sky will light up your life.

Will you receive my gift... or just walk away?

The illumination will shine one day on the ripples of
the mesmerizing ocean waters, tantalizing your eyes so
that you may seek inner wisdom....only to wither away
once the eyes shut and the sun rises once again.

Alas, I am full.

Proudly I display my magic between the tree
branches, high above a mountaintop or on the
horizon to catch your attention once more.

To look,
To seek,
To see your reflection in me.
The brilliance that waits for you is patient,
Your time will come.

I am always here waiting for someone, perhaps you,
to notice that you can shine high above the world and
radiate in the whole universe, your sparkling heartbeat,
your illuminating brilliance of divine love.

You were always whole.

~ Gloria Coppola

*"And perhaps what made her
beautiful was not her appearance
or what she achieved,
but in her love, and in her courage,
and her audacity to believe:
No matter the shadows around her,
light ran wild within her,
and that was the way
she came alive and it showed up
in everything."*

– Morgan Harper Nichols

Conclusion

*"Your unconscious database outweighs the conscious on
an order exceeding ten million to one. That unconscious
database is the source of great wisdom and power."*

~ Michael Gelb

You may not realize it but you just experienced a soul alchemy
journey with us.

Something happened within each of us as we began this
journey together and something evolved that we didn't expect
or know about until the state of dissolution shifted our stories
to gold, the higher calling.

As you read these stories perhaps you related, maybe you
were shocked or felt compassion and inspiration. Every
emotional frequency at a quantum level of awareness takes us
through miraculous changes to the deep inner healing even as
we read .

The ripple effect and beauty of the process happens

unconsciously at first; then we begin to transmute the awareness to alter our reality as we heal and integrate through inner transformation all in divine right order.

I aligned with all these women, situations and circumstances as the alchemic journey I chose matched the frequencies necessary for this project. I walked in every shoe as I supported each woman in their writing process. I came to know them differently and I cried. These were not tears of sadness but fluid, like liquid gold because I was privileged to see their golden gifts.

Many of us went through another dark night of the soul to honestly and more deeply accept our true authentic self . We went through states of fear, forgiveness, responsibility and evolving into a new light, purpose and deeper soul love.

This is soul alchemy! This is the courage it takes to align with the soul's purpose and journey from external power to authentic inner strength.

You experienced these golden gifts, the magic and sovereignty. You were part of this creation, molding the shattered pieces even when you felt shaken. You found the power within to climb higher and heal your life to follow the Divine Plan. For when goddesses and angels are united our super powers emerge and we all stand strong together.

Gratitude extended to each and every one of you.

~ Gloria Coppola, soul alchemist, publisher *Powerful Potential and Purpose*

Become a Published Author!

Gloria Coppola and Candy Lyn Thomen focused on a vision they were shown and said YES. Guidance said to meet up at Lake Louise, Canada. Out of that journey, *Powerful Potential and Purpose Publishing* was born to align heart-centered writers who have a bold, courageous and important message for the world.

Gloria and Candy's skillsets and attention to detail go above and beyond. They provide a personal, intuitive touch to help you reach your full potential and fulfill your soul purpose to help others.

- Over 80 years of combined experience
- Soul-focused, creative writing coaching
- Intuitive, custom cover design and book layout
- Editing and proof-reading
- Amazon and KDP research
- Expert Marketing
- One-of-a-kind, personal touch

Do you have a desire, a message, a heart-centered journey that must be told? Your time to be an author is NOW!

www.PPP-Publishing.com   gloria@gloriacoppola.com
PPPPublishingUS@gmail.com

Powerful
Potential *and* *Purpose*

PUBLISHING